HABAKKUK
before
BREAKFAST

LITURGY, LAMENT, *and* HOPE

Brian J. Walsh
     and the Wine Before Breakfast community

Also available from Books Before Breakfast

St. John Before Breakfast

HABAKKUK

before

BREAKFAST

LITURGY, LAMENT, *and* HOPE

Brian J. Walsh
and the Wine Before Breakfast *community*

 CASCADE *Books* • Eugene, Oregon

HABAKKUK BEFORE BREAKFAST
Liturgy, Lament, and Hope

Cascade Books
An Imprint of Wipf and Stock Publishers
199 W. 8th Ave., Suite 3
Eugene, OR 97401

www.wipfandstock.com

PAPERBACK ISBN: 978-1-5326-9293-2
HARDCOVER ISBN: 978-1-5326-9294-9
EBOOK ISBN: 978-1-5326-9295-6

Cataloguing-in-Publication data:

Names: Walsh, Brian J., author.

Title: Habakkuk before breakfast : liturgy, lament and hope / Brian J. Walsh.

Description: Eugene, OR: Cascade Books, 2020.

Identifiers: ISBN 978-1-5326-9293-2 (paperback) | ISBN 978-1-5326-9294-9 (hardcover) |
    ISBN 978-1-5326-9295-6 (ebook)

Subjects: LCSH: Bible. Habakkuk—Study and teaching.

Classification: BS1585.55 .W45 2019 (paperback)

Manufactured in the U.S.A.   1/07/2020

Cover and text designer: Katie Yantzi
Cover image: Gregory "Iggy" Spoon
Text set in Book Antiqua

In memory of
Gregory "Iggy" Spoon
March 18, 1968 – March 17, 2015

Contents

INTRODUCTION

It began, as so many of these things do, with a hunch.

If you are not going to use the lectionary, then how do you determine the texts that will shape your worship life together? Through prayer, cultural discernment, pastoral attentiveness, and a listening for what the Spirit may be saying to the community.

In other words, you go with a sort of spiritual hunch.

Where might we as a Wine Before Breakfast community dwell for the six weeks from the beginning of the second semester to Lent? Is there a particular text that we might need to hear? A word from God that might be calling us? A biblical author who will lead us more deeply in our ongoing wrestling match with God? Is there a certain place that seems to be an entry into the Story for us at this time? A biblical book that might serve to shape our imaginations, give voice to our longings, resonate with our lament, and engender a hope in the midst of it all?

For some reason, Habakkuk came to mind. Here was a prophet who stood in that rich covenantal tradition of no-holds-barred spiritual honesty. Here was a prophet for whom everything seemed to be going wrong and nothing transpired as expected. Justice seemed to be turned on its head, and with it everything that he thought that he knew about God. Both lament and complaint were at the heart of this prophet's vision, and that seemed to be right for the Wine Before Breakfast community in January of 2015.

It is quite the thing to pastor a community that gathers at 7.22 on Tuesday mornings. That is a spiritual discipline at the best of times, and the dead of a Toronto winter is usually about as far from the best of times as you can imagine. Not only is it cold, it is dark. And for some reason it seemed that the cold darkness of this prophet of collapse, this prophet of deep anguish and confusion, was a darkness that we had to enter.

Why? Why would we choose Habakkuk when we didn't have to do so? Well, part of my hunch was that Habakkuk might have a word for a post-Christendom church. You see, folks at Wine Before Breakfast have neither illusions about nor nostalgia for Christendom. Indeed, many of our folks bear Christendom as an oppressive weight on their backs. "Been there, done that, and have the scars to show for it." No, Christendom is something well lost. Might Habakkuk, a prophet of endings, have a word to say at the end of Christendom? Might he help us get beyond a cheap "Three cheers for the death of Christendom!" (admittedly, my default position), and open the door for us to lament this death and the unravelling of a body of certainty that could no longer serve us? Wine Before Breakfast is a decidedly post-Christendom kind of community. Maybe Habakkuk can give us the language to deal with what is now lost, in anticipation of what is now being born.

Sounded good. Seemed like a careful discernment of the community and how the ancient prophet might speak anew into our midst.

Habakkuk didn't seem too impressed with my hunch. The prophet didn't seem inclined to speak into my construal of post-Christendom. No, Habakkuk wanted to go deeper than my hunch had imagined. Maybe it was the cold and the dark of that winter, maybe it was the deep struggles of members of the community, or maybe it was the escalation of violence that we were confronting from the streets of Toronto to the deserts of the Middle East … but something was going on with Habakkuk that blew apart my expectations. The prophet seemed to have something else in mind.

Habakkuk Before Breakfast is the second offering from our little publishing venture, Books Before Breakfast. Following up on the 2014 offering, *St. John Before Breakfast*, this book offers a glimpse into the worship life of our community. In these books we bear witness, we offer a testimony.

Each of the six chapters of this book begins with a **reflection**. This is the invitation into the text. Every week I send a pastoral email to the Wine Before Breakfast community that invites us to begin to meditate on the text for that week. This is a sort of spiritual priming of the pump; a beginning reflection on the biblical text that invites the community both into the world of the text and to a worship shaped by that text.

After the reflection, our musical director, Deb Whalen-Blaize, offers a brief **musical/liturgical comment**. The experience to which this book bears witness is an aural and visual experience. "You had to be there." But most people reading this book weren't there. You didn't taste the bread and wine, you didn't hear the prayers, you didn't dwell in the silences, you didn't shed any tears. You didn't have to see through the darkness or the snow to get to church that morning. You didn't look into the eyes of a sister or brother as you passed the peace together. And, at the heart of it all, you didn't hear the music, nor did you sing. So we want to offer some comment on what happened on each of these Tuesday mornings. More specifically, we want to reflect on the music for each service and how the songs that we used resonated with the text in such profound ways that they also set off resonances deep within ourselves.

At Wine Before Breakfast we have a rich tradition of opening and closing each service with a song from the world of contemporary pop, rock, and folk music. These songs, together with the hymns for congregational singing,[1] are chosen the same way the lectionary got chosen in the first place. Through a process of prayer, discernment, listening. And what we are looking for is precisely the resonance that I just mentioned. If the prophet is standing on his watchtower to see how God will respond to his complaint, then doesn't Bob Dylan's "All Along the Watchtower" suggest itself? Or if Habakkuk is describing the violence of empire, and twice speaks "of human bloodshed and violence to the earth, to cities and all who live in them," then might it not be time to hear the band perform Bruce Springsteen's "My City of Ruins"? So what happens when these songs get played in worship? How do the songs help to shape our hearing of scripture, our experience of the Spirit, and our prayers?

After the musical/liturgical comment, each chapter proceeds to offer four more components of each service: the **gathering of the community**, the **homily**, the **prayers of the people**, and then the **prayer after communion**.

Wine Before Breakfast is a participatory community. Various people have written the prayers, curated the services or prepared the homilies. This means that this book, like our worship life together, offers a feast made by many hands. Just as our breakfast is provided by members of the

---

1   We use as our hymnal *Common Praise* (Toronto: Anglican Book Centre, 1998). All hymn numbers refer to this book.

Bread Guild, muffin makers, and a multiplicity of cooks bringing different dishes for our culinary enjoyment, so also is our worship multi-voiced. Students, housing workers, theologians, street pastors, parish priests, campus ministers, and others all play a role in setting the table, serving the bread and wine, opening up the word for our hearing, and leading our prayers.

Amanda Jagt provided the first round of copy-editing on this book. Laura Bast served as the managing editor and Katie Yantzi did the design work on both the cover and the layout of the book. *Habakkuk Before Breakfast* wouldn't be in your hands without the good work of these three members of the community.

But there is one member whom we want to remember. Sometime during this series on Habakkuk the community received a gift of art, elements of which grace the front and back cover of this book. Greg "Iggy" Spoon was a First Nations brother from Northern Ontario. He had seen some pretty bad times in his life. And for some reason he kind of adopted Wine Before Breakfast as part of his extended community. Iggy would show up sometimes at the back of the chapel, sometimes downstairs waiting for us when we came from worship to breakfast. And Iggy was a very fine artist. One day he showed me a picture that he was making for the community. A bottle of wine, a chalice, a loaf of bread, some fruit, an open book, a music staff with the name of our community written on it, and … a butterfly, symbol of transformation. This was his gift to the community. But it wasn't finished yet. He didn't know what to write on the bottle. What vintage of wine? Or might he put the time and place of our services? Or might he (reaching into his satchel for a bottle) put "Kelly's" on the bottle? Kelly's is the cheapest and most potent wine that homeless folks drink. "I don't know, should we put Kelly's on that bottle?" Iggy asked. Yes, I replied. That's exactly what should go on that bottle. If Wine Before Breakfast is about anything then surely we should be about taking such a terrible wine, a wine of such heartbreak and sorrow, and asking Jesus to make that a holy wine, a sacramental wine, the wine of the new covenant in his blood.

A few weeks after our series with Habakkuk was finished, our brother Iggy fell terribly ill. There was a 24-hour vigil at his bedside in the Intensive Care Unit. While he was in that unit we placed his picture on the communion table and someone would take the bread and the wine on Iggy's behalf. "The body of Christ, broken for Iggy." "The blood of Christ, shed for our brother Iggy." At 11.00 am on March 17, 2015, our brother Iggy returned to his Creator. We were deeply honoured to receive the gift of his art from this brother. And we were humbled to be counted as his friends. We dedicate this book to his memory. Iggy didn't hear any of the sermons in this book. He didn't need to. He already knew.

Brian J. Walsh
Eastertide 2016

1 VIOLENCE AND DESTRUCTION: HOW LONG?

HABAKKUK 1.1-11

1 The oracle that the prophet Habakkuk saw.

2 O Lord, how long shall I cry for help,
     and you will not listen?
   Or cry to you "Violence!"
     and you will not save?
3 Why do you make me see wrongdoing
     and look at trouble?
   Destruction and violence are before me;
     strife and contention arise.
4 So the law becomes slack
     and justice never prevails.
   The wicked surround the righteous —
     therefore judgment comes forth perverted.

5 Look at the nations, and see!
     Be astonished! Be astounded!
   For a work is being done in your days
     that you would not believe if you were told.
6 For I am rousing the Chaldeans,
     that fierce and impetuous nation,
   who march through the breadth of the earth
     to seize dwellings not their own.
7 Dread and fearsome are they;
     their justice and dignity proceed from themselves.

8   *Their horses are swifter than leopards,*
        more menacing than wolves at dusk;
        their horses charge.
     Their horsemen come from far away;
        they fly like an eagle swift to devour.
9   *They all come for violence,*
        with faces pressing forward;
        they gather captives like sand.
10   *At kings they scoff,*
        and of rulers they make sport.
     They laugh at every fortress,
        and heap up earth to take it.
11   *Then they sweep by like the wind;*
        they transgress and become guilty;
        their own might is their god!

Reflection
Donne, Dylan, Cohen, Tennyson, and Habakkuk: Ringing in the New Year … Sort of
Brian Walsh

If you have ever been to Russet House Farm,
you likely have heard our bell.

Taken from a one-room school house years ago,
and gifted to us by some dear neighbours,
our bell calls people to break bread together,
sometimes punctuates the events of the day,
and can, if necessary, ring out a warning,
    calling all to gather in the face of crisis.

"Send not to know for whom the bell tolls," John Donne instructs,
    "it tolls for thee."

I'll never forget the first time I heard such a bell toll,
the first time I heard a bell mournfully ring
in the face of death.

Truth be known, it scared the crap out of me.

A few days ago, we were given little bells
   upon entering a church for a funeral.
Bells, we were told, mark passages,
   and they announce sacred moments.
As we made our farewells to our friend
   we marked this as such a passage, such a sacred moment.
And so we were invited to ring our bells.
If good old Peter, Paul and Mary "had a bell" they
   "would ring out a warning,"
and then they would
"ring out … the love between my brother and my sister,
   all over this land."
      ("If I Had a Hammer")

Bob Dylan, many years later, sang,

   ring them bells …
   for the time that flies
   for the child that cries
   when the innocent dies …
      ("Ring Them Bells")

while Leonard Cohen solemnly intoned,

   ring the bell that still can ring,
   forget your perfect offering,
   there is a crack, a crack in everything,
   that's how the light gets in.
      ("Anthem")

Bells – they're everywhere.

And so we have "rung in" the new year.

Maybe Alfred, Lord Tennyson captured it best:

   Ring out, wild bells, to the wild sky,
   The flying cloud, the frosty light:
   The year is dying in the night;
   Ring out, wild bells, and let him die.

   Ring out the old, ring in the new,
   Ring, happy bells, across the snow;

The year is going, let him go;
Ring out the false, ring in the true.
    ("In Memoriam")

Maybe that's what we need to do at the beginning of a new year:
ring out the false, ring in the true.

Of course, that's easier said than done.

The false is insidious,
it holds us captive,
blinds us to its own falsehood,
    and even leaves us imagining that it is true.
So Tennyson gets specific.

Ring out the feud of rich and poor,
Ring in redress to all mankind.

Ring out the want, the care, the sin,
The faithless coldness of the times ...

Ring out false pride in place and blood,
The civic slander and the spite;
Ring in the love of truth and right,
Ring in the common love of good.

Ring out old shapes of foul disease;
Ring out the narrowing lust of gold;
Ring out the thousand wars of old,
Ring in the thousand years of peace.

Ring in the valiant man and free,
The larger heart, the kindlier hand;
Ring out the darkness of the land,
Ring in the Christ that is to be.

Here's the thing.
You can't "ring in the Christ that is to be"
unless you ring out
    the old, the false,
    the lust, the violence,
    the oppression, the slander,
    the spite and pride.

That's why we need poets, songwriters, and prophets.

At Wine Before Breakfast, we hang out with a lot of poets,
ancient and contemporary.

From the Psalmists to U2,
    from Isaiah to Cohen,
    from Jeremiah to Dylan.

Whether it is the poetry of the prophets,
    or the poetic parables of Jesus,
and the lyric prose of Paul,
we know our imaginations need poetry
to be set free.

So … what happens if we ring in the new year with the
    ancient prophet, Habakkuk?

What happens if we listen in on Habakkuk ringing out
    the old, the false,
    the lust, the violence,
    the oppression, the slander,
    the spite and pride of his time,
and allow his prophetic voice to resonate
    in our own times,
    with our own lives?

Let's see what happens.

Musical/Liturgical Comment
Deb Whalen-Blaize

It is bleak as we open this ancient prophecy, and, frankly, it pretty much
stays that way. And so, in the bleakness, in the darkness, I mused on a
few songs about trying to see clearly. I wrote a message to Brian asking
what he thought of using U2's "When I Look at the World," to which
he responded, "Too optimistic." I had expected a confirming reply but
instead I got a sobering one. And so I dug deeper for songs about the state
of a broken world.

Prelude	Anthem *Leonard Cohen*
Postlude	Ring Them Bells *Bob Dylan*
Hymns	Weary of All Trumpeting *#582*
	Wind Upon the Waters *#408*
	Our Darkness *Taize*
	O Healing River *#578*

I don't know why I bother looking beyond Leonard Cohen at all, sometimes. Because upon my second scouring of lyrics, I came across "Anthem," and there were the lyrics we needed to hear:

Ring the bell that still can ring
Forget your perfect offering
There is a crack, a crack in everything
That's how the light gets in.

That last line could also be seen as optimistic, except that it does not undo the soberness of there being a crack in everything. Habakkuk begins his abrasive and painful oracle by telling God that everything is broken, and demanding to know what exactly the Holy One is going to do about it. Here is an important resonance. Cohen says that there is a crack in everything and maybe Habakkuk is trying to find that crack, trying to find that light in the darkness.

Our hymns echoed this desire to mend the brokenness and find healing, calling to God for his Spirit to come and soothe the ache and put the pieces back together. As we read through this passage full of carnage due to hubris, power-mongering, and the absence of God, we sang that we were "weary of all trumpeting, weary of all killing, weary of all songs that sing promise, non-fulfilling," as we begged for God to "shower down upon the dry earth of my soul." Remaining in this place of longing in the dark, we reached for a simple Taize chant for communion: "Our darkness is never darkness in your sight / the deepest night is clear as the daylight." As we ate the bread and drank the wine we moved from a deep blindness to a gentle version of "O Healing River."

Bob Dylan's "Ring Them Bells," with its clear symmetry with Cohen's "Anthem," provided a poignant close to our worship. Both Cohen and Dylan have bells to ring and so do we. Our prayers employed lines from Tennyson's large work of poetry, "In Memoriam A.H.H." "Ring out" we prayed. "Ring out the old, ring in the new," knowing that as we did so we "rang out the grief … the want, the care, the sin." Wearied by a world on its side, we were called to ring those bells, signalling that we would not give up.

> Ring them bells for the blind and the deaf
> Ring them bells for all of us who are left
> Ring them bells for the chosen few
> Who will judge the many when the game is through?

So we began our sojourn with Habakkuk. So we rang in the new year.

> Our darkness is never darkness in your sight
> The deepest night is clear as the daylight

The Gathering of the Community
Brian Walsh

What time is it?
Time to ring the bells that still can ring.

What time is it?
A time of war and violence.
The dove is never free.

What time is it?
A time when the killers in high places
still say their prayers out loud.

What time is it?
It is early, very early, on a Tuesday morning.

So why are you here?
Every heart, every heart to love will come,
but like a refugee.

Then come, dear friends,
come as refugees to love,
come and bring your broken offerings,
    your broken hearts,
    your broken bodies,
    your broken spirits,
    your broken lives.

What time is it?
It is time to tell the truth.

What time is it?
It is time to abandon deceit.

What time is it?
It is time to ring the bells, cracked and broken.

What time is it?
It is time to worship.

Homily
Habakkuk in Epiphany?
Brian Walsh

Wasn't that supposed to be Isaiah?

Weren't we supposed to hear this morning,
    "Arise, shine, for your light has come,
    and the glory of the Lord has risen upon you"?
Isn't that what Epiphany is all about?

Doesn't Isaiah go on to proclaim to defeated Israel,
    "Nations shall come to your light,
    and kings to the brightness of your dawn"?

So what is Habakkuk doing in Epiphany?

While Isaiah calls the people to "lift up your eyes and look around"
    to see their children coming home
    and the nations flocking to the light of Israel,
Habakkuk complains that all he can see is
    wrongdoing and trouble,
    destruction and violence,
    strife and contention.

So what is Habakkuk doing in Epiphany?

The same thing that Herod is doing in Epiphany.

You see, that whole story of the Magi from the East
    coming to see the newborn Messiah
is book-ended by paranoid Herod,
    fearful of a threat to his sovereignty,
    and brutal with infanticide to eradicate that threat.

Habakkuk knows all about violence.
He is burdened by it, weighed down, demoralized and angry.
Violence is everywhere!
And it is invariably the violence of the powerful against the powerless,
    the violence of the rich against the poor.
This is the violence to which the covenant people have been reduced.

And he figures that all of this is somehow God's business.
He doesn't just shrug it off with a defeated pessimism.
No, he puts it all in the face of God.

"How long shall I cry for help,
    and you will not listen?
How long shall I cry to you, 'violence!'
    but you will not save?

Why do you make me look at all of this pain,
    this endless suffering,
    this unspeakable cruelty,
and not allow me to avert my gaze?

Torah – the law that should protect the vulnerable,
    the law that should be the foundation of justice –
is so compromised, so ineffectual, so controlled by the powerful
    that justice is impossible,
    and no one can get an honest hearing in court!

The righteous, those little ones who seek justice,
    those who still dream of your kingdom,
are surrounded, hemmed in, corralled, and the system is stacked
    against them.

When will all of this end?
When, O God, will you do something about it?"

That resonate with anyone in the room?

Anyone here this morning who has had enough of the violence?
    Who just can't bear to watch the news anymore?
    Who has seen the devastating impact of oppression in the lives of the
        vulnerable?
    Who has shed too many tears – of rage, of despair, of loss?

Anyone here who faces a new year with a sinking feeling of more of the
    same?
Anyone here who has seen enough and, damn it, God doesn't seem to
    be listening?

Or let me put it this way.
Is there anyone here who is more taken with Rachel weeping for her
    children
    than with wise men bringing gifts from the East to baby Jesus,
        just before he and his parents become refugees from Herod?

If so, then maybe there is room for Habakkuk in Epiphany.

But it only gets worse.

God's devastating answer to Habakkuk's lament seems to say,
    you haven't seen nothing yet.
The violence and destruction,
    the strife and oppression
that you see at home
    will call forth a terror that you couldn't have imagined.
Open your eyes and look around.

I know, I know, you think that you have seen enough.

But look beyond your walls,
    look beyond your homemade violence

– as real and as devastating as it is –
   and see.

Be astonished! Be astounded!
This is so terrible you wouldn't believe it if I told you.
So look and see what is happening.

The very ground is shifting in the affairs of the nations.
The old foes, the old empires, the old geo-political dynamics
   are all irrelevant,
   all about to be swept away by a force that no one saw coming.
And all of the old rules
   – of diplomacy and tribute, of détente and alliances –
are swept away as quickly as this nation will rise.

Here come the Chaldeans,
   defeating Assyria, Nineveh, Haran, and Egypt
   one after another at lightning speed.
No wonder they scoff at kings and make sport of rulers.

These are a fierce people who strike dread and fear
in the hearts of all who are in their path.

There is no buffer between them and you, O Judah,
there is no alliance that will save you,
there is no distance that is beyond their reach.

They come for one reason and one reason only:
   for violence,
   for plunder,
   to take you captive.

In Judah the law may have become slack,
   but the Chaldeans are a law unto themselves,
   they recognize no justice or human dignity beyond themselves,
   their own might is their god.

So Habakkuk, that is what the covenant God has to say in response to
   your complaint.

Are you upset that I don't see?
Are you angry that I don't listen?

Well I do see and I have listened,
and the Chaldeans – as fiercely evil as they are – are my response.

You are tired of the violence and oppression
    the lawlessness and injustice of the covenant people?
Then I will deal with the covenant people
    with a violence and oppression,
    a lawlessness and injustice
    that goes beyond your worse nightmares.

Epiphany?
Light to the nations?
Wise men bearing gifts from the East?

Hell no.

Judgment.
Exile.
And a violent people bearing death from the East.

Why go to Habakkuk in January of 2015?
Why do we need to hear this voice speaking to us
    at this time in history?

Is it because ISIS is a force as unexpected
    and as violent as the Chaldeans?
Is it because we have seen horrendous things
    done by desperate and violent people?
Well, yes. That is part of the reason that we need to listen to Habakkuk.

But maybe there is more.
Maybe we need to listen to Habakkuk
because he spoke of a turn of history that was unthinkably destructive
    and violent,
and maybe we are at a similar historical juncture.

Maybe there is a violence about to be unleashed in our time,
    the violent fruit of imperialism and colonialism,
    the violence that is born of radical climate change
        and environmental destruction,
    the violence of a world of desperate inequality,
    the violence of an economic system tottering towards collapse.

And maybe, just maybe, entering into Habakkuk's struggle with God,
  Habakkuk's struggle with justice,
  Habakkuk's struggle with empire,
might open up vision and even hope for us.

Things were bad for Habakkuk and Judah,
but they were about to get a whole lot worse.

Things are bad for our civilization and for the post-Christendom church,
but, I'm pretty sure, they are about to get a whole lot worse.

My hunch is that Habakkuk might be the prophet
  to help us find our way.

So let's take the next few weeks to test out that hunch.

Oh yeah, one other thing … Happy New Year.

Prayers for a New Year
Amanda Jagt
(with excerpts from Tennyson's "In Memoriam A.H.H.")

Ring out, wild bells, to the wild sky,
the flying cloud, the frosty light:
the year is dying in the night;
ring out, wild bells, and let it die.

**It is a new year, O Lord,
yet we struggle
to hold onto the hope
that you are working in our days.**

(prayers for the new year)

Ring out the old, ring in the new,
ring, happy bells, across the snow:
the year is dying, let it go;
ring out the false, ring in the true.

All of our hurt, our pain, our fear,
all of our questions,
all of our bodies and hearts,
our minds and spirits,
we bring to you.

(prayers for comfort and healing)

Ring out the grief that saps the mind,
for those that here we see no more;
ring out the feud of rich and poor,
ring in redress to humankind.

Destruction and violence are before us,
strife and contention arise
in our city and in the world,
and we yearn for justice.

(prayers for justice)

Ring out the want, the care, the sin,
the faithless coldness of the times;
ring out, ring out my mournful rhymes,
but ring the fuller minstrel in.

For not joining in your song,
O Lord, forgive us.

(prayers of confession)

Ring out false pride in place and blood,
the civic slander and the spite;
ring in the love of truth and right,
ring in the common love of good.

Always you are with us
and always we are loved.

(prayers of gratitude)

Ring out old shapes and foul disease;
ring out the narrowing lust of gold;
ring out the thousand wars of old,
ring in the thousand years of peace.

Give us wisdom in waiting, O Lord,
wisdom in wading through mystery,
and wisdom in acting,
today and in all the days ahead.

(prayers for wisdom)

Ring in the valiant and the free,
the larger heart, the kindlier hand;
ring out the darkness of the land,
ring in the Christ that is to be.
Amen.

Prayer After Communion

All your works praise you, O Lord.
And your faithful servants bless you.

Gracious God,
we thank you for feeding us
with the body and blood of your Son, Jesus Christ.

May we, who share his risen body,
live his risen life;
we, who drink this cup,
bring life to others;
we whom the Spirit lights,
give light to the world.
Keep us firm in the hope
you have set before us,
so that we and all your children
shall be free,
and the whole earth live to praise
your name;
through Christ, our Lord. Amen.

2 OF FISH HOOKS, JUDGMENT, AND WATCHTOWERS

HABAKKUK 1.12-2.1

12 Are you not from of old,
   O Lord my God, my Holy One?
   You shall not die.
   O Lord, you have marked them for judgment;
      and you, O Rock, have established them for punishment.
13 Your eyes are too pure to behold evil,
      and you cannot look on wrongdoing;
   why do you look on the treacherous,
      and are silent when the wicked swallow
      those more righteous than they?
14 You have made people like the fish of the sea,
      like crawling things that have no ruler.

15 The enemy brings all of them up with a hook;
      he drags them out with his net,
   he gathers them in his seine;
      so he rejoices and exults.
16 Therefore he sacrifices to his net
      and makes offerings to his seine;
   for by them his portion is lavish,
      and his food is rich.
17 Is he then to keep on emptying his net,
      and destroying nations without mercy?

2.1 I will stand at my watchpost,
      and station myself on the rampart;

> *I will keep watch to see what he will say to me,*
>   *and what he will answer concerning my complaint.*

Reflection
Fishers of Men?
Brian Walsh

I will make you fishers of men,
fishers of men,
fishers of men.
I will make you fishers of men,
if you follow me ....

Remember that from Sunday School?

Picking up on Jesus' call to his fishermen disciples,
the song invites the children to also become fishers of "men,"
presumably evangelizing their playmates in elementary school.

A lot of us might be a tad uncomfortable with that song.

Maybe we started chuckling when we realized that the hand actions
that accompanied the song were so anachronistic –
    mimicking casting a fishing rod with a lure,
    rather than throwing out a net.

But I wonder if maybe the song misses the meaning of the metaphor.

I mean, the song assumes that Jesus is talking about evangelism,
    about rescuing folks from their sin and damnation.
But show me one fish who ever thought
    that being pulled out of the water
    – whether by hook or net –
was good news!

So what is really going on with that metaphor
    of capturing people in nets?

Well, as far as I can see, this is a metaphor used in the Hebrew Bible in
    only one way – as an image of judgment.

In Psalm 10.9, Amos 4.2, Jeremiah 16.16, and this week's reading from
    Habakkuk 1.15, the metaphor is consistently employed to describe a
    violent judgment on (wait for this) ... the people of God.

Tell that to the Sunday School kids.

"Hey kids, if you want to follow Jesus then you get to bring his violent
judgment on all the good folks at church! Isn't that great?"

Well Habakkuk wasn't too impressed.

"Are you crazy?" the prophet seems to complain to God.

"This makes no sense! You are going to use those treacherously violent
and evil Chaldeans to treat your people – who are bad, but not *that* bad!
– like fish to be plucked from the sea? These folks love violence so much
that they bless and make sacrifices to their weapons! And you are going
to sit back and let them destroy us and all the other nations without
mercy?"

Nope, Habakkuk won't have it, and he sure won't make a nice little song
for the children out of this vision.

Rather, he's going to stand and watch and wait to see what God will say
in response to his rebuke.

So what am I saying?

Well, for starters, let's dump that sentimental Sunday School song.

Then let's have the courage to look God's crazy judgment
    straight in the face.
Maybe we should dare to perceive such judgment in our own time.
And if we don't like it, then maybe we need to have
    the chutzpah of Habakkuk,
        both in our discernment of the times
    and in our relationship with God.

Martyn Joseph has a song called "Not a Good Time for God."
Kind of resonates with Habakkuk, when you think about it.

And in her haunting song "Après Moi," Regina Spektor sings that in the
    face of it all, "I must go on standing ... I'm not my own, it's not my
    choice."

Habakkuk says that he will stand on the watchtower
to see how God will answer his protest.

So let's replace "Fishers of Men" with Joseph and Spektor.

Let's respond to the terrorism, the pain, and the horror with lament.

Musical/Liturgical Comment
Deb Whalen-Blaize

Lamenting God's lack of action, Habakkuk gets right into describing the torment of the righteous. Helpless little creatures snatched up in the net of the enemy, surrounded by chaos, and God doesn't seem to be lifting a finger.

Martyn Joseph is a friend to the Wine Before Breakfast community and we have often reached for his music in our worship. He is a troubadour whose lyrics are incisive, incendiary, and prophetic. Martyn's hard-hitting "Not a Good Time for God" almost seems to be written with Habakkuk in mind.

It's not a good time for God
It's not a good time
Atheists deplore him
Hedonists ignore him
Men with bombs adore him

Agnostics rarely need
Think tanks never heed
Orthodoxy creeds him
It's not a good time for God

A world where God doesn't fit. God is nowhere in this world. Both Martyn and Habakkuk are describing a frightening world in which there seems to be little promise of the righteous making the world right again. They are at God's mercy. But there's not much mercy around in a world characterized more by God's absence than by his presence. In fact, if God ever did show up, there wouldn't be much room for him anyway. "Agnostics rarely need… Think tanks never heed… Orthodoxy creeds him." It's not a good time for God.

The two Taize chants we sang during communion stitched together the beginning and end of the service. This time we chanted:

> By night we hasten in darkness
> To seek for the living water
> Only our thirst lights us onward
> Only our thirst lights us onward

And then ...

> Wait for the Lord, whose day is near
> Wait for the Lord, be strong, take heart

Both of these songs make me think of a tired, miserable trudge. In the dark. The long drawn out notes and minor melodies connect me viscerally with times when I have had to push myself onward well after I have wanted to give up. The thing is, I never feel alone when I sing these songs. I feel connected to all the other voices who sing, who have sung, and who will sing these words. I am not the only one on this difficult path. There are many of us here, led only by our thirst. A thirst for righteousness, for justice, for this kingdom that God began building but is sometimes so far out of reach that we hardly believe it was ever there to begin with. We share this thirst, and we urge each other, with every step, to not give up. To wait for the Lord, to be strong, and to take heart.

Regina Spektor knows this trudge. In the original recording of "Après Moi," she interrupts the line "I must go on standing" by a guttural grunt right after that first word, as if she's not only willing herself with all her might to stay on her feet, but that in the process she has just taken a blow to the gut. She is facing the adversity. "I – ugh! – MUST... go on stand ... ing." We ended our service with this defiant, willing, and dreary dedication.

> I must go on standing
> You can't break that which isn't yours
> I must go on standing
> I'm not my own
> It's not my choice

We willed our collective self to stand with Habakkuk on the ramparts, waiting and watching for God. We willed ourselves to go on standing in this world with no time or place for God, his eyes too pure to behold such evil. Beyond reason or hope, sometimes the will does not give us a choice at all. We must go on standing. Watching. Waiting.

Prelude	Not a Good Time for God *Martyn Joseph*
Postlude	Après Moi *Regina Spektor*
Hymns	Our Cities Cry to You, O God *#591*
	How Long *Stuart Townend*
	By Night We Hasten *Taize*
	Wait for the Lord *Taize*

By night we hasten in darkness
To seek for the living water
Only our thirst lights us onward
Only our thirst lights us onward

Wait for the Lord, whose day is near
Wait for the Lord, be strong, take heart

The Gathering of the Community
Amanda Jagt

God, it's not a good time for you.
It's not a good time for us, either.

Morning has broken
but still it feels like night.

(silence)

To you the darkness is not dark
and the night is bright as the day.

You came to us in love.
We come now to you.
We come to cry.
We come to rejoice.
We come to sing.
We come to worship.
We come to speak.
   Will you listen to us, O God?
We come to listen.
   O God, will you speak to us?

Homily
Let Me Tell You About Fish Hooks
Jacqueline Daley

Last fall, I made a decision to end my employment with Canada's largest social housing landlord after about ten years of service.

I made the decision after coming to the end of hope that this instrument, in its current form, and me as an agent of it, could have any meaningful or sustainable impact on the lives of the city's most marginalized.

After ten years of seeing too many lives unravel under the weight of poverty, isolation or by the deadly force of a gun, I saw the need for my own recovery from all that I saw. I need recovery from what I have seen.

Consider Nadine, a young mother who waited ten years for a three-bedroom unit where she could finally house her twins (early teens) whom she was separated from for over seven years while she worked two jobs so she could afford to sponsor them to come to Canada from Grenada.

I saw Nadine's joy when her twins arrived; she proudly showed them off everywhere she went. But in less than six months, Nadine's joy vanished into anguish, after her kids were apprehended by the Children's Aid Society (CAS).

The CAS, a warehouse whose caseload consists 41% of African Canadian children, who represent only 8% of the city population.

In less than six months, Nadine lost her twins to CAS; she would eventually lose her job from missing work to attend all the hearings. Her mind would soon follow, and then her housing, the unit she had waited ten years for and spent all her savings to furnish like a palace.

I saw too many seniors, my grandmothers' generation, who just died alone, often from a fall, often over piles of clutter. With no family, no next of kin, no kids, friends, or church to come looking for them, they eventually died, not from the fall, but from dehydration.

Their cries for help unable to penetrate the heavy door that is supposed to offer protection from fire.

They are often discovered when the odour from their decaying bodies begins to interfere with their neighbours' right to reasonable enjoyment of their poor-quality housing.

I can't forget the eyes of 16-year-old Romain, whom I saw on an ordinary Friday afternoon hanging out in the lobby.

He looked younger than his age; he had dark eyes that sparkled with innocence and potential.

When I inquired why he was not at school, he responded, "Miss, school is not for me." I responded, "Okay, school is not for everyone. Come see me on Monday at 10 am and I will try to hook you up with a job."

Romain never arrived. He was gunned down within 24 hours of our conversation. His death added (but who is counting) to over 400 African Canadian young people (the majority of them male) killed in our neighbourhoods during my ten years of service.

I saw the works of the enemy who catches lives, like Nadine's, with a hook, and drags them with his net of injustice.

I saw and smelled our grandmothers' decayed bodies being taken away without mourners, while countless mourning mothers, like Rachel, continue to weep over the senseless slaughter of their sons.

It's the same weeping I heard yesterday from grandparents, who dealt with the sudden loss of a beloved grandchild, and from the families of recent victims of terror wherever terror strikes.

This morning we continue our journey in the book of Habakkuk. Like me, this guy is seeing a lot; he is desperately seeing something very different from what others are seeing.

Habakkuk refuses to stay blind to the injustice of his time and he refuses to shut up in the face of the silence of God. He has sharp and penetrating eyes to see God's justice clearly.

So with forceful words, he has the courage to voice the things he sees with his complaint to God, the same source who gave him those sharp eyes to see all the troubles.

You see, Habakkuk's biggest problem is that he can't seem to reconcile two irreconcilable realities: the God he knows as the Holy One, Eternal, Creator, and Righteous Judge over against the injustice he sees and understands to be the judgment of this very same God.

In pain and confusion, Habakkuk asks, *"Why do you look on the treacherous and are silent when the wicked swallow up those more righteous?"*

God, why do you remain silent in the face of pain, death and injustice?

Perhaps that is why we continue to gather so early on Tuesdays, hopeful for eyes like Habakkuk – sharp enough to see God's justice and sharp enough to muster up the courage to voice our protest wherever the hook of injustice is felt.

At the end of our passage we see Habakkuk standing at his watchpost, waiting, keeping watch to see if there is a response from God. He is not interested in hearing – he knows seeing is believing. He wants to *see* something radically different.

So perhaps at the very least, that is what this prophet of pain is inviting us to do. Perhaps Habakkuk is calling us to enter into a much deeper level of seeing, speaking, and anticipating the justice of God.

You and I are invited to see God's truth wherever we are planted. Whether in our work, study, neighbourhoods, or churches, we are being invited to see and speak God's justice.

Perhaps we can take this disturbing reading as our wake-up call, our alarm clock to awaken us from the dangers of both blindness and silence.

It's easy to stay blind to injustice, especially when the pay, perks, and privileges are working for us. Especially when injustice is wrapped in shallow niceness and politeness. Especially when the hierarchy of victimhood includes us at the top of the ladder, with those who look like us, sound like us, and are familiar faces in our orbit.

Habakkuk is offering us something more risky, as he stands with eyes wide open to God's justice in a world where justice has gone south. He stands, with the pain and anguish of an injustice that he is directly affected by, with the audacity and courage to ask, why is this so?

I believe he has invited us to do likewise. Habakkuk reminds me that there is no recovery from my ten years working with Canada's largest landlord. There is no exit, no going back, from what I saw with my own eyes.

As a matter of fact, the only way out is to stay in (stay in the pain), so that we (you and I) can have a close-up view of the damage caused by the hook of injustice from within – within the lives of Nadine, Romain, and isolated, decomposing seniors.

I believe Habakkuk offers us something wonderful to feed on – a rare form of resolve we need in our time. The resolve to wait with radical resistance; the resolve to resist blindness and silence that is often mistaken for acceptance.

Habakkuk gives us permission to persist in seeing, speaking, and working in full anticipation that God's justice will prevail, with the confidence expressed in the words of Martin Luther King, Jr.: "The arc of the moral universe is long, but it bends toward justice."

Prayers of the People
Luke McRae

God, we come before you to declare and to plead.
We declare that in us and about us is night
and we plead for the morning.

Your eyes are too pure to look on evil.
Are you looking elsewhere?
Turn your face towards us.
Your creation is caught, ensnared.
Our hearts and minds and bodies are bound.
Our lives are consumed as fuel.

Lives are cut short, carved up,
gobbled down, tossed away;
and your satisfied people talk only of recipes and ovens.

(we confess the sins of our world and of ourselves)

Was this what you had in mind?
Are these cruel flames your refineries?
Why are you silent
while the wicked swallow up
those more righteous than themselves?

Bomb the ovens, turn the tables, defend us!
We are weak, for we have no ruler.
We would be vindicated now, with power and glory.
We want a king over us.
Then we will be like the other nations.

We are redeemed but easily recaptured.
We remember the fine food of the land we left behind.
We have been called.
May we not abdicate.
In our zeal,
let us not raise up new tyrants.

(prayers for peace and guidance)

Our Father, if there is no legion of angels in Gethsemane tonight
how will your kingdom come?
If we are devoured before dawn
how will your will be done?
If you turn your face from evil
how can it be on earth as it is in heaven?

Keep us close a little longer.
Give us today our daily bread.
And we will stand here to keep watch.

Prayer After Communion

Amanda Jagt

Precious Lord,
you are our light in the darkness.
As we go forth today, you go with us.

Help us to go forth into the world in peace,
to remember that we are not our own,
to be of good courage,
to hold fast that which is good,
to render to no one evil for evil,
to strengthen the faint-hearted,
to support the weak,
to help the afflicted,
to honour all people,
to go on standing,
to love and serve you,
and to rejoice in the power of the Holy Spirit.
Amen.

THE RIGHTEOUS LIVE BY FAITH, BUT WEALTH IS

3 TREACHEROUS

HABAKKUK 2.2-11

2 *Then the Lord answered me and said:*
   Write the vision;
      make it plain on tablets,
      so that a runner may read it.
3 *For there is still a vision for the appointed time;*
      it speaks of the end, and does not lie.
   If it seems to tarry, wait for it;
      it will surely come, it will not delay.
4 *Look at the proud!*
      Their spirit is not right in them,
      but the righteous live by their faith.
5 *Moreover, wealth is treacherous;*
      the arrogant do not endure.
   They open their throats wide as Sheol;
      like Death they never have enough.
   They gather all nations for themselves,
      and collect all peoples as their own.

6 *Shall not everyone taunt such people and, with mocking riddles, say*
      about them,

   "Alas for you who heap up what is not your own!"
      How long will you load yourselves with goods taken in pledge?
7 *Will not your own creditors suddenly rise,*
      and those who make you tremble wake up?
      Then you will be booty for them.

8   *Because you have plundered many nations,*
      all that survive of the peoples shall plunder you —
    because of human bloodshed, and violence to the earth,
      to cities and all who live in them.

9   *"Alas for you who get evil gain for your house,*
      setting your nest on high
      to be safe from the reach of harm!"
10 *You have devised shame for your house*
      by cutting off many peoples;
      you have forfeited your life.
11 *The very stones will cry out from the wall,*
      and the plaster will respond from the woodwork.

Reflection
Standing on the Watchtower ... With Habakkuk, Dylan, and Hendrix
Brian Walsh

"There must be some way out of here," said the joker to the thief,
"There's too much confusion, I can't get no relief."

So begins Bob Dylan's iconic and enigmatic song,
    "All Along the Watchtower."
    Looking for some escape,
    some release from the confusion all around us.

The joker can find no humour in the situation,
    no way to turn it on its head,
    no path of deconstruction.

This joker perceives a culture of theft and expropriation,
    a profound devaluation of all things:

"Businessmen, they drink my wine, plowmen dig my earth,
None of them along the line know what any of it is worth."

It is the thief, however, who sees things in perspective:

"No reason to get excited," the thief, he kindly spoke,
"There are many here among us who feel that life is but a joke.

But you and I, we've been through that, and this is not our fate,
So let us not talk falsely now, the hour is getting late."

We have walked the path of irony,
    the path that copes either through evasion or cynicism.
And so, discerning that the time is late,
the joker counsels that we abandon falsehood,
    abandon all that would cloud our vision,
        all that would avert our gaze.

If the hour is getting late, if the time is short,
    then it is time to be vigilant, eyes wide open,
    taking our place on the watchtower:

    "All along the watchtower, princes kept the view
    While all the women came and went, barefoot servants, too.

    Outside in the cold distance a wildcat did growl,
    Two riders were approaching, and the wind began to howl."

Dylan offers a poignant sketch,
    an incomplete narrative,
    an evocative vision,
    an apocalyptic portent
        of the times.

The time was the autumn of 1967.
Dylan released "All Along the Watchtower" on December 27
    of that year.

Less than a month later, on January 21, Jimi Hendrix entered the studio to
begin work on his own version of Dylan's song.

While Dylan recorded "Watchtower" in one day with the support of
bass and percussion, Hendrix would be in and out of various studios for
months with an ever-changing cast of musicians and producers.

The result was stunning.

Dylan was, in his own words, "overwhelmed" by what Hendrix accomplished with his song, and adopted Jimi's version in his own performances
from the first time he heard it.

There was a spaciousness to the Hendrix interpretation
that deepened its impact,
and heightened its sense of apocalyptic immediacy.

Why?
Why did Jimi Hendrix's version of this song take it to a new level of
meaning – indeed, to a new level of cultural significance beyond what
Dylan had accomplished?

Was it Jimi's virtuosity?
No one would compare Dylan and Hendrix as guitar players.

Was it Jimi's attention to detail, not satisfied to release a song after one
day in the studio?

Or was there something else going on here?

Might it be that when this song,
      written by a brilliant beat poet–inspired artist
      in the folk scene of New York City,
gets interpreted by an African American artist living at the same time,
      the meaning changes?

You see, when you start talking about economic exploitation,
      stripping people of their land,
      the devaluing of all things – even other human beings,
      a world of barefoot servants,
      and a profound sense of loss, anger, and dread,
then maybe a black artist sees, feels, and experiences things
      that a white artist does not.

Maybe the view is different from that watchtower,
      depending on who you are
      and what you and your people have suffered.
Maybe that fearful "growl" in the distance is more terrifying
      and that foreboding "howl" of the winds of change more ominous.

But that is what a great song makes possible:
opening up different vistas,
      different interpretations,
      a deepening of truth.

Dylan undoubtedly had the biblical metaphor
      of the "watchtower" in mind when he wrote this song.

Read Isaiah 21.8-9:

"Upon a watchtower I stand, O Lord,
continually by day,
and at my post I am stationed throughout the night.
Look, there they come, riders,
horsemen in pairs."

The allusions in Dylan's song are clear.

And haven't we heard from Habakkuk 2.1:

"I will stand at my watchpost,
and station myself on the rampart;
I will keep watch to see what he will say to me,
and what he will answer concerning my complaint"?

So what is going on here?

In Isaiah and Habakkuk we meet prophets who are watching.
    They are both watching Babylon,
    an empire that will implode.
    And they both see this collapse
    long before the evidence merits such a judgment.

Bob Dylan composes a song that employs this prophetic metaphor
    to interpret the world in a very different age and time.
    He is also watching an empire that will implode.

Jimi Hendrix interprets Dylan's song a mere month later
    in a world that is the same as Dylan's,
    but as seen through the eyes of the African American experience
    of that same imploding empire.

An ancient text offers a prophetic interpretation of the world,
    that text is interpreted some 2,600 years later,
    and then interpreted again at the same time
    from a different perspective.

An interpretation of an interpretation of an interpretation.

Some years later U2 joined the long list of artists who have offered their
    interpretation of "All Along the Watchtower." And while, musically,
    U2 didn't really do anything to the song, Bono did add another verse:

"All I got is a red guitar,
Three chords and the truth.
All I got is a red guitar,
The rest is up to you"

Admittedly, these lines are not quite up to the poignancy
    of the original.
And yet, in their simplicity, they are also profoundly true.

Three chords and the truth.
We have the song.
We have the text.
We have these words.

Dylan had the prophetic text,
    the rest was up to him.
Hendrix had Dylan's song,
    the rest was up to him.
We have the prophetic text,
    and we have Dylan's song,
    and we have Hendrix's interpretation;
    the rest is up to us.

That's what we do on Tuesday mornings at Wine Before Breakfast.
We take seriously that it is up to us to interpret this ancient poetry.
It is up to us ... in community,
    to interpret these words,
    to stand on the watchtower
        with Isaiah and Habakkuk,
        and also with Dylan and Hendrix,
    in the face of an imploding empire,
    and see what God will do.

That's at least part of what it means to dwell in the scriptures
    at 7.22 in the morning.
And maybe if we do that deeply enough,
    we too might find our place among the prophets,
    we too might become a prophetic community.

Musical/Liturgical Comment
Deb Whalen-Blaize

Here we are, up on the ramparts watching the kingdom crumble under the weight of injustice, and Bob Dylan is singing "All Along the Watchtower." Scenes of siege from a number of fantastic films and television series flood my memory as Dylan captures this moment of watching and waiting with one of his most evocative songs. Surveying the carnage below from the vantage point of that watchtower, the artist balances patience with contempt, while still finding a word of mercy in this devastating hour of need. The potency of Dylan's siege scene, in three short verses, sets us up for a service in which we recall our steely resolve to wait for the Lord.

And then God shows up and tells Habakkuk to get his pen out and listen carefully. He's in charge of the rest of the chapter. God reminds us of the vapid emptiness of pride and arrogance, and that cultural practices born of these things are unsustainable and will not last. He warns: "Alas for you who heap up what is not your own! … Because you have plundered many nations, / all that survive of the peoples shall plunder you." And this is actually sweet music to our ears. This terror and oppression will not last. Dylan sums it up like this:

> "No reason to get excited," the thief, he kindly spoke
> "There are many here among us who feel that life is but a joke.
> But you and I, we've been through that, and this is not our fate,
> So let us not talk falsely now, the hour is getting late."

That unjust heap is going to topple. And probably soon.

After Bob Dylan, the community sang "Let Streams of Living Justice," one of my favourite hymns.

> Let streams of living justice flow down upon the earth;
> Give freedom's light to captives, let all the poor have worth.
> The hungry's hands are pleading, the workers claim their rights,
> The mourners long for laughter, the blinded seek for sight.
> Make liberty a beacon, strike down the iron power,
> Abolish ancient vengeance; proclaim your people's hour.

We sing these words when we need hope. To remind us that while we don't understand how God works, we know he loves justice and wants what is good. We sing of our helplessness and dependence on God and his timing. We sing of our hope in him.

Despite our desire for the vanquishing of our enemies, and all injustice with them, what do we do while evil wreaks havoc around us? How do God's promises play out while we suffer? Where is God while we are suffering? Is he really such along way off?

God promises us that his Spirit is near. Always. The role of God's spirit is to comfort, to commiserate, and to remind us of the strength in us to overcome. We are reminded that we are created in his image and no amount of injustice can take that away from us. That the whole world can burn at the hand of evil, but God's love does not change. God's love longs to renew and restore what evil would destroy. The hard part is knowing what to do until that renewal actually happens. It is hard to trust these promises in the midst of suffering. And so together our community sang "It Is Well with My Soul." For me, this particular verse hits home:

> For me, be it Christ, be it Christ hence to live:
> If Jordan above me shall roll,
> No pang shall be mine, for in death as in life
> Thou wilt whisper thy peace to my soul.

"You and I have been through that, and this is not our fate," the Holy Spirit whispers. It can be hard to sing things as bold as "it is well with my soul" when things do not feel well with your soul. But when you can hear the Holy Spirit whispering softly that the truth is beyond the devastation that surrounds you, or, better still, that the truth lies untouched and whole within you, you can sing beyond your emotions. Sing, in faith, the things you hope to feel later.

Through communion we sang "Healer of Our Every Ill," meditating on God's power to heal through comfort and hope. It is important to have songs that speak to those in pain now without pushing them to "delight in the Lord" at once! A community needs to be able to plead with God to provide us with peace that carries us beyond our fear and hope, beyond our sorrow, while we are in the thick of it. It is good to be reminded that God's character and promises are present even in the greatest despair.

God's promise in Habakkuk is that there is still a vision for the appointed time and it does not lie. This allows us to cope in a world that is not yet reconciled to God's kingdom. The watchtower is not a place of dwelling. We eventually leave our watch for someone else to take over, and we head back down to real life among the ruins. And while the chaos plays

Prelude	All Along the Watchtower *Bob Dylan*
Postlude	The Servant's Ace *Joe Pug*
Hymns	Let Streams of Living Justice *#575*
	It Is Well with My Soul
	Healer of Our Every Ill *#612*

out around us, we can still make choices that honour God's desire for our lives. Choices that further his kingdom, and make this world look more as he intended. Joe Pug frames a picture of such confidence in "The Servant's Ace":

> There's a bird, fair and gold,
> whom my owners do hold.
> She refuses to make them a sound.
> How it pains them to think
> that for me she does sing
> While I carry their riches around.
>
> I might work in their fields,
> bear them their meals
> I might carry the letters they send.
> There's a treasure, I know,
> buried deeply below
> That will shatter the shovels of men.

God's truth is life-giving. It makes the most beautiful music. It inspires us to hang on for another day, to continue the watching and waiting, wherever we are. When we walk in confidence of who God is and who he made us to be, when we live out the love we are given, and act in the power and strength that comes with God's love, we can stand up to a lot – even the evil and injustice that happen around us every day. God's word will stand, and it will outlast every treachery, even our own. In such confidence we hold on, and we watch and wait, no matter how the wind howls.

The Gathering of the Community
Marcia Boniferro

God, we wait all along the watchtower.

Your kingdom,
We long for it.

Your renewal,
We ache for it.

Your transformation,
We wait for it.

You say: "Write the vision!"
You say: "Make it plain!"
You say: "If it seems to tarry, wait for it;
it will surely come, it will not delay."

Let us not talk falsely now, the hour is getting late.
Help us to watch, to wait, to try to stay awake!

Homily
Standing on the Watchtower
Brian Walsh

"All I got is a red guitar,
Three chords and the truth.
All I got is a red guitar,
The rest is up to you."

So adds Bono to Bob Dylan's "All Along the Watchtower."

All I've got is an ancient text,
that has the ring of truth.
All I've got is an ancient text,
the rest is up to you.

Or, perhaps, the rest is up to us.

Here we are, three weeks into Habakkuk,
up to our necks it seems.

Here we are, deep into the burden that this prophet saw.

And seeing through his eyes has had terrible resonances.

We have seen, unexpectedly I confess, the violence of our world,
    indeed … let us name it …
    the violence of a virulent distortion of Islam,
    crying out from this prophecy.

We have seen, unexpectedly I confess,
    people pulled away as if by fish hook,
    indeed … let us name it …
    in the failed culture of Toronto Community Housing,
    crying out from this prophecy.

We have seen, quite expectedly I confess,
    that we live in the midst of systems,
    ideologies, economies, and cultures of violent idolatry,
    that make sacrifices to their gods,
    and it is the most vulnerable and defenseless who are sacrificed.

So we have taken our stand with Habakkuk on the watchtower.
We have resolved to not talk falsely,
    to tell the truth,
    and to put our complaint in the only place where it might get
    a response:
    at the very throne of God.

We are on this watchtower with Habakkuk,
    with all who have suffered enough and demand an answer,
    with our sister Jacqueline who has seen enough,
    with Dylan and Hendrix,
    with Bonhoeffer, Romero, and Dorothy Day,
    and if you look at the crowd up here with us
        just down the rampart a little … do you see him?
    there is St. Paul over there, standing on Habakkuk's watchtower.

Here's the deal, the Holy One replies,
    I know that it is hard to see any way out of here,

I know that it is hard to get your bearings,
I know that it all seems so violently hopeless,
I know that it is hard to see through the smoke
and through your tears,
    but this is not our fate,
    there is still a vision,
    so let me paint it large for you.

There is still a vision of an end to this horror,
    and it does not speak falsely.
I know, I know that it can't come too soon.
I know that you are impatient.
I know that it seems to be taking so damn long,
    but wait a little longer, my friends,
    it will not delay.

It is a vision that lies just beyond the range of normal sight;
    you will have to strain your eyes a little,
    but once you see it, it will become as clear as day.

So take a look.
Look at the proud.
Look at those who wield this destructive violence.
Look at the 1% who will soon own more than 50% of all the wealth.
Take a good look.
What do you see?

They project such an ethos of ease and comfort.
They appear to be so secure and confident.
They appear to have everything under control.

But look more closely.
Wealth is treacherous.

    Yes, yes, we know that!

But do you also see that such arrogance cannot endure?
Can you see that this is a world that can only implode?
Can you see that an economy of insatiable consumption
    is like Death that has never had enough?
Can you see that such an economy will swell and bloat
    until it explodes?
Can you see that a global capitalism of exploitation and injustice
    will necessarily call forth rebellion?

Can you see that if you heap up what is not your own,
    if you set up a world economy of plunder,
    if you secure that economy through a geo-politics of bloodshed,
    and if you continue to do violence to the earth and to cities and to
    those who live in them,
    then the whole thing is going to rebound on you?
Does it take too much just to open your eyes and see all of this?

And if you can't see it, then might you be able to hear it?

If you listen closely enough,
    can't you hear the cry of the stones in the walls
    and the plaster responding from the woodwork?

We may be blind to what is going on,
    but the rest of creation is not.
We may simply see the shiny architecture of opulence
    in the construction boom all around us,
    but the building materials know better.
And so they, like all of creation, cry out in travail,
    call out in protest to how they are employed in service of idolatry,
    bear witness against a culture of treacherous wealth
    in the face of poverty,
    call out a shameful housing policy that builds condos for the rich,
    while 72,000 households are on the waiting list
    to get into affordable housing.

Shame, cry out the two-by-fours and the drywall. Shame.

But you and I, we've been through that, and this is not our fate.

Because, you see, hidden in this vision,
    almost drowned out by this deconstruction of the empire,
    set in contrast to the proud in all of their disquiet,
there is another word.

St. Paul noticed it.
St. Paul knew that this was the heart of the matter.
St. Paul knew that while the empire was collapsing,
    there was one anchor in the storm,
    one thing that you could build everything on
    in the reconstruction project of our culture, our economy, our lives.

"Look at the proud!
Their spirit is not right in them,
but the righteous live by faith."

The righteous live by faith.
Those who would seek justice live by faithfulness.
Faith, faithfulness, is at the heart of the matter.

But there is a question here.
There is, not surprisingly, a matter of interpretation,
    both in Habakkuk and when St. Paul cites Habakkuk in Romans.

Whose faith?

Our translation this morning offers one interpretation:
    "The righteous will live by *their* faith."

Now, here is an interesting thing.
That interpretation of Habakkuk is well grounded in the Septuagint,
    that is, in the ancient Greek translation of the Hebrew text.
In fact, we could say that the Greek translation is itself an interpretation.

The Masoretic text, however (that is, the Hebrew text), is less clear.
    "The righteous will live by faithfulness" is how it reads.

Faithfulness.
Whose faithfulness? Their own?
Or the faithfulness of the very God who has been addressed
    from the watchtower?

How can you trust that this vision,
    though taking such a long, long time,
    will come to pass?
How can you hang on with righteousness in the face of wickedness,
    with justice in the face of injustice?
Because the one who gives you this vision,
    the one who calls you to such righteousness, such justice,
    is the faithful one.
Live in the security of this faithfulness.

Whose faithfulness?
It can go either way in Habakkuk,
    and I think that St. Paul intentionally embraces both interpretations.
At the very foundation of his letter to the Romans,

Paul writes,
"For in the gospel the justice of God
    is revealed through faith for faith;
as it is written, 'The one who is just will live by faithfulness.'"

Through faith for faith.
Through the faithfulness of God
    is born the faithfulness of God's people.
So if you are to live in justice,
        if you are to have vision in the midst of the collapse,
        if you are to see clearly through the smoke and the tears,
            you must be embraced by the faithfulness
            of the One who will not let his creation go;
            you must allow that faithfulness
        to make you into a faithful people.

At the heart of it, God is saying, "trust me."
As you have eyes to see the endgame of the proud,
    trust me to be faithful.

Keep faith and you keep God.
Keep faith and you will see clearly.
Keep faith, embrace a righteous justice,
    and the vision will open up to you.
Keep faith, hold each other in faith;
    indeed, hold our world in faith,
        and we just might see hope on the other side of the catastrophe,
        hope at the end of history.

Prayers of the People

Nate Wall

God of Zion,
we have stood at the watchpost
with the prophet,
with sister and brother,
with singer and poet,
and we have waited
to see what you will say.

Let us not talk falsely now:
we have seen far too much.
There must be some way out of here;
we can't get no relief.

We have seen
nations plundered and villages slaughtered,
empires built and pockets lined,
terror leveraged and voices silenced.

But you, O God, have spoken of the end.
Please, do not lie.
You seem to tarry.
Why make us wait?
How long, O Lord?
How long?

(prayers for justice, for peace, for truth)

God of Zion,
we have stood at this watchpost,
but even in our waiting,
we have grown so, so weary.
But still, you have answered.

We have a vision of your justice, writ large:
a meal of freedom, a body once broken,
a voice that says, "Peace be with you."

So let us not talk falsely now.

Our wealth has been treacherous
but you keep faith when we are false.

The proud trust their securities
but your steadfast love endures forever.
Businessmen drink our wine
but you make our cups overflow.
Death would swallow us alive
but you have become our bread.

Because we believe that
you have turned your face to us,
we turn our face to you again.

(prayers of return, of confession, of reorientation)

God of Zion,
we stand at this watchpost
with the prophet,
with sister and brother,
with singer and poet,
and we wait to see a new city.

Let us not talk falsely now:
**we have come
to see Mount Zion,
the city of the living God,
the heavenly Jerusalem,
the home of righteousness,
the healing of the nations,
and your dwelling with us.**

And we offer ourselves as living stones.
**Build us a city that can't be shaken.
Make us the righteous who live by faith,
and haste the day when our faith will be sight.**

Prayer After Communion
Marcia Boniferro

God,
Your kingdom come.
Your will be done.

On earth!
As in heaven.

And so, we say together:
**Glory to God
whose power, working in us,
can do infinitely more
than we can ask or imagine.
Glory to God from generation to generation,
in the Church and in Christ Jesus,
for ever and ever. Amen.**

4 IDOLS, GLORY, AND SILENCE

HABAKKUK 2.12-20

12 "Alas for you who build a town by bloodshed,
        and found a city on iniquity!"
13 Is it not from the Lord of hosts
        that peoples labor only to feed the flames,
        and nations weary themselves for nothing?
14 But the earth will be filled
        with the knowledge of the glory of the Lord,
        as the waters cover the sea.

15 "Alas for you who make your neighbors drink,
        pouring out your wrath until they are drunk,
        in order to gaze on their nakedness!"
16 You will be sated with contempt instead of glory.
        Drink, you yourself, and stagger!
    The cup in the Lord's right hand
        will come around to you,
        and shame will come upon your glory!
17 For the violence done to Lebanon will overwhelm you;
        the destruction of the animals will terrify you –
    because of human bloodshed and violence to the earth,
        to cities and all who live in them.

18 What use is an idol
        once its maker has shaped it –
        a cast image, a teacher of lies?
    For its maker trusts in what has been made,

though the product is only an idol that cannot speak!
19 *Alas for you who say to the wood, "Wake up!"*
    to silent stone, "Rouse yourself!"
    Can it teach?
    See, it is gold and silver plated,
        and there is no breath in it at all.

20 *But the Lord is in his holy temple;*
    let all the earth keep silence before him!

Reflection
From the Violent Clamour of Empire to Silence Before the Creator God: Still Listening with Habakkuk
Brian Walsh

As we continue our reading of Habakkuk we meet these words:

> "… because of human bloodshed, and violence to the earth,
>   to cities and all who live in them."

Twice.

Twice we meet the same words in God's response to Habakkuk.

The tables will be turned on the empire,
    God assures the aggrieved prophet.
What goes around, comes around.
The proud will fall from their elevated places.
The plunderer will be plundered.
The violence at the heart of your economy will revisit you.
And the terror of your rule will rebound upon you
    in a terrorism that will know no bounds.

Why?

> "… because of human bloodshed, and violence to the earth,
>   to cities and all who live in them."

Bloodshed and violence beget bloodshed and violence.

That is an ironclad law of the universe.

Human bloodshed.
Violence to the earth.
Violence to the cities.
Violence to those who live in them.

And the oracle says it twice.

The geo-political violence of empire
   always, always, always
is manifest in ecological violence
and a violence at the heart of urban life.

Same old, same old.

But the God of shalom,
the God of justice,
the God of creation,
the God of love
   will have nothing of it.

And so the good news for Habakkuk
is that this whole idolatrous house of cards will fall.
And great will be its fall.

But there is more:
"The earth will be filled
with the knowledge of the glory of the Lord,
as the waters cover the sea."

Judgment is never the last word.
Judgment is always a word on the way.
A clearing of the way for a better word.

A world filled with violence,
overflowing in blood,
will be transformed.

Glory replaces shame.
Intimate knowing replaces objectified control.
Silence overtakes the cacophony of empire.

   "But the Lord is in his holy temple;
   let all the earth keep silence before him!"

Sometimes, in the face of such things,
the best thing to do is to shut up.

Musical/Liturgical Comment
Deb Whalen-Blaize

> Well I got bones beneath my skin, and mister
> There's a skeleton in every man's house
> Beneath the dust and love and sweat that hangs on everybody
> There's a dead man tryin' to get out

We humans sure know about misery, don't we? Adam Duritz of Counting Crows paints a pretty bleak, but frank, picture in the song "Perfect Blue Buildings." I remember hearing this song for the first time as a teenager – probably when my life was at its most bleak. It was comforting to know that this strange reality, not being quite happy with what was going on around me, was a situation shared by many. I would look around me and everything looked fine. But there was so much insecurity underneath it all. Such unhappiness. Unsettledness. There was decay beneath that smooth finish. We cannot separate destruction from life. Even as we grow and heal and become wiser, things decay, and people die, and pain returns again and again. The second half of Habakkuk 2 seems to really hone in on this: life amidst death. The juxtaposition is a hard reality. We may be ready to start sweeping up the rubble from the destruction around us, but it's not over yet, and knowing there's more to come makes us just wanna pack up and move on altogether.

I don't really know what these blue buildings are that Duritz sings about. Overpriced condos of questionable quality? A rehab facility? Hotels in a resort town? He talks about being asleep in perfect blue buildings, "beside the green apple sea," wanting to get some sweet oblivion. Whether he's talking about literally being asleep or just existing among the walking dead, there are too many of us that can relate to this desire for oblivion. To escape. And this is normal. The dream is a momentary respite we use to take a break from reality. But if it lasts too long, we lose touch with reality. Submitting to the desire to ignore our everyday reality leads to all sorts of unhealthy possibilities, not the least of which is that walking deadness. If life is going to be meaningful, we need to find a way to be able to live among the rubble, rather than just painting over everything and pretending it's fine. Because life can happen amidst decay and ruin.

After such a bleak opening tune, the community stood to sing "Be Thou My Vision." I always get excited responses when I tell people we're singing this tune. It is an opportunity to declare where our focus needs to be, sung to a most beautiful Irish melody. We can't allow ourselves to be dragged into the mire of hopelessness. We must, with discipline, keep our eyes on God – which sometimes means looking for him in unexpected places. God will enlighten our darkness and show us the way forward. Allowing God to show us how to live in the brokenness is the best alternative to denying it or succumbing to it. Our lives will forever be figuring out this tension, and God offers to show us the way. "But the earth will be filled with the knowledge of the glory of the Lord, as the waters cover the sea." (Habakkuk 2.14)

And then we sang about the kingdom. Rather than dreaming about a perfect escape, we envisioned God's kingdom. We filled our minds with images of restoration and wholeness.

> The kingdom of God is justice and joy
> For Jesus restores what sin would destroy
> God's power and glory in Jesus we know
> And here and hereafter, the kingdom shall grow
>
> The kingdom is come, the gift and the goal
> In Jesus begun, in heaven made whole
> The heirs of the kingdom shall answer his call
> And all things cry glory to God all in all

While partaking of the elements in this Eucharist, we sang through some poignant chants, once again from Taize. Over and over again we reminded ourselves, and one another, that:

> The kingdom of God is justice and peace
> And joy in the Holy Spirit
> Come, Lord, and open in us
> The gates of your kingdom

Thank God for the gift of the Holy Spirit. Thank God that she has a voice that breaks through the gloom, even if it's just to remind us of the promise that the ways of destruction will not last. That change will come. Even a gentle voice can be a thing of great power. I find the last few verses in Habakkuk 2 very interesting. There is talk about too much trust being put in idols and how they don't respond to commands because they are nothing more than fashioned items. Humans can shape objects, but not

Prelude	Perfect Blue Buildings *Counting Crows*
Postlude	My City of Ruins *Bruce Springsteen*
Hymns	Be Thou My Vision *#505*
	The Kingdom of God *#631*
	Bless the Lord, My Soul *Taize*
	The Kingdom of God Is Justice and Peace *Taize*

provide them with sentient life, the way God did when he shaped us. Habakkuk also talks about all the earth keeping silent before the Lord in his holy temple – because no one tells God what to do. He is the Creator, not the created. We may as well save our breath. But when God speaks to us, when we hear the Holy Spirit's voice, we can be brought to life and filled with hope. If we hear that voice and remember God's promise, we may be able to find within us the strength to hold on for another day.

And so Springsteen's "My City of Ruins" seemed an appropriate way to close the service around this scripture. Like Duritz, Springsteen sings of ruin, though his response to a difficult reality is different. Springsteen doesn't acquiesce to the hardship and contemplate the escape of oblivion. Rather, Springsteen sounds more like the Holy Spirit, calling to the skeleton in Duritz's house. He has something to say to the bones beneath our skin, covered in dust and love and sweat, trying to get out. He calls out, "Rise up!" My friend Dave performed this song in this service. We were his choir, joining the call to rise up. He set us off singing about rebuilding God's kingdom from the brokenness around us "with these hands." We ended up on our feet by the end of this tune, determined not to escape into oblivion, but to rebuild and rise.

This song has such power, especially when there is a chorus of voices joining in that refrain. The Holy Spirit can speak with many different voices. She wants to be heard. Sometimes she sounds like Springsteen. Sometimes she sounds like my friend Dave. Sometimes she sounds like the person sitting next to you. Sometimes she sounds like you.

Bless the Lord, my soul
And bless his holy name
Bless the Lord, my soul
He leads me into life

***

The kingdom of God is justice and peace
And joy in the Holy Spirit
Come, Lord, and open in us
The gates of your kingdom

The Gathering of the Community
Prayer of Confession
Brian Walsh

Holy God, Maker of all,
Have mercy on us.
Jesus Christ, servant of the poor,
Have mercy on us.
Holy Spirit, breath of life,
Have mercy on us.

Let us in silence
remember our own faults and failings.

(silence)

It doesn't get much worse than this,
getting a little oblivion,
skeletons in our closets,
a crippling attitude of need.

I'm messed up,
caught in meaninglessness,
help me, I'm falling.

May God catch you,
Christ be the Truth for you,
and the Spirit heal you.

Amen, thanks be to God.

It doesn't get much worse than this,
getting a little oblivion,
skeletons in our closets,
a crippling attitude of need.

We're messed up,
caught in meaninglessness,
help us, we're falling.

May God catch you,
Christ be the Truth for you,
and the Spirit heal you.

Amen, thanks be to God.

Homily
Idolatry and the Systems of Bloodshed
Thea Prescod

My parents met and fell in love in their home country of Barbados. Right after their honeymoon, however, they flew to Canada and started their life here. The transition was dramatic. They moved from a largely agrarian community to a city, and they moved from being in the racial majority to being racial minorities. The story of their first few years here is full of the hardship and strength. Mom particularly has a few memorable tales of dropping her resumé off at businesses where HR would mysteriously never receive them. She quickly learned that she always got job interviews when she mailed in her resumé, and never got interviews when she dropped it at the front desk in her dark-skinned glory. Those were the stories I grew up hearing about Canada. In my family, we had to talk a lot about race and its impact on our lives. But, my family always talked about racists and never about racism. It never occurred to me that they could be separate things.

We went to a church that reinforced this way of existing in the world. Sins were personal. Choose which way you want to act, and ask God for his strength to live well. If enough of us Christians lived holy lives, the world would become a better place.

We talked a lot about "the earth being filled with knowledge of the glory of the Lord" while never talking about how our very city of London, Ontario, Canada was built by bloodshed, and founded on both iniquity and inequity.

I had been hanging around Sanctuary a while before I realized that our cities, our nation, was built by bloodshed. Early on in my time here, I was attuned to see the individual sins as being, well, individual. My focus on personal pieties left me viewing the acts of violence that we saw in the clinic where I served as a nurse without context. Gary beat up Frank. How awful that Gary would act like that, probably because he had finished an entire bottle of Kelly's Sherry (which is, incidentally, our communion wine this morning). Smith hurt his girlfriend Sally. I should get her some domestic violence resources and encourage her to leave. Casey was beat up last night by the cops. It's awful that there are these bad apples in the system.

Eventually, that paradigm broke down. I came to realize it was utterly unworkable and unrelated to the reality I was seeing day today. That shift was devastating. The slow, dawning realization that there's a deep vein of violence in Canadian society, particularly violence towards Indigenous People and their lands, was distressing and destabilizing for me, so deeply so that I still haven't recovered.

Alas for Canada, we've made the first peoples of this land drink, pouring out racism and imperialism like poison and then sneering at their shame.

We've poured out poison, and then clucked at their drunkenness.

We've poured out poison, and then taken children, saying, "They'll be better off if they grew up in a stable, non-indigenous home."

We've poured out poison and then said, "Look at the brokenness of this people group who are without Christ."

We missed that it is precisely our Canadian culture, with our church-based residential schools, that was, often as not, the culture that was truly without Christ.

And I haven't even gotten to our destruction of forests and wildlife.

I grew up hearing about how, if you're travelling around the world, it's important to pin a Canadian flag to your backpack. The worst possible thing would be if someone mistook you for an American. Common wisdom was, everyone loves Canadians while everyone loathes the US. Imagine my surprise when some of my friends started backpacking around Central and South America. In town after town they were told about Canadian mining companies destroying their habitat and bullying their Indigenous Peoples into silence. I hear the same from friends raised in northern First Nations communities. They tell me of their homes being forcibly relocated to clear the way for mines and dams. Of lands where they used to hunt being decimated by polluted earth and waters. They tell of a system of intimidation and bribes used to perpetuate voiceless-ness and powerlessness in the face of corporate greed.

I don't have to point out the idols, do I? We know where the bodies are buried. Racism, greed, and violence are just the tip of the iceberg. This whole country was built on shaky ground.

There are subtler idols, though. Systems we've created with our own hands, ones that we're now hoping will pull a Pinocchio, come to life and save us.

I have spent hours of my life caring for friends who've been brutalized by the Toronto police. Besides bandaging and icing, I've documented bruis-es in the shape of boots, sent in complaints that largely went unanswered. There is a deeply violent streak in our police force which – combined with classism, racism, and cronyism – poisons even individual cops who want to do good. That said, I have friends in domestic violence situations, and I desperately want the police to do something about their partners. De-spite all of the evidence I've seen of its inherent brokenness, I somehow dream that state violence could repair broken homes with broken bodies.

Canada's very name is based on mishearing, misunderstanding, and co-opting indigenous culture. From the earliest days, our cities' existence depended on us shoving people northward towards less productive soil and climes while taking strategic sites on waterways: Toronto, Ottawa, Montreal, Quebec City, all built on this. For centuries our government systematically tried to destroy First Nations culture through the *Indian Act*, residential schools, and the child welfare system. And yet, I still look for governmental policy change. I pray for just laws. I tell myself that our government is just made of people, many of whom want to do right, be-cause acknowledging the powers upon which our system has been built is just too dispiriting, and it leaves me lacking imagination about what hope looks like. So I write letters to the empire, hoping for stone to rouse.

And despite the ways in which the church has consorted and colluded with these powers, I still look to her to lead us into a new way of being.

Despite a lifetime of evidence that the church has been gilded with the silver and gold of empire, I persist in asking her if she has anything left to teach.

But in the midst of it all exists a promise. Somehow, the knowledge of God's glory will saturate the earth. These cities, built on blood shed by marginalized peoples, will receive a fresh infusion: this time, of a blood that heals, that redeems. A blood that brings life and dignity, instead of tearing it all apart. Blood given by choice and shed by the most powerful, instead of being gouged from those who have the least left to give.

I've become fundamentally incapable of imagining how we move from here to there. From a system founded on iniquity in a way that seems irreparable to a city where the Lamb is the light for all peoples. I live my life deeply compromised by my interaction with the dead systems we create, yet unable to walk away from them completely. I end up overthinking, worrying, caught by how my privilege both blinds and implicates me. I don't know, so often, how I'd even measure the lesser of all the evils that surround me.

And then I remember the voice of comfort in my life, the truth that holds it all together. God speaks, and says, "The vantage point from my temple allows me to see all of human history. I know where we've come from and where we're going. It's time for you to shut up, and to start listening."

Prayers of the People
Joyce Mak

The Lord is in his holy temple,
let all the earth keep silence before him.

(silence)

Where do your promises begin, Lord?
Where do they end?

For the earth will be filled —

**every broken and weary nation,
every bloody and battered town,**

every lonely and torn apart home,
every trampled and empty heart,

with the knowledge of the glory of the Lord –

written on our hearts,
scratched across the sky,

as the waters cover the sea.

You are in your holy temple,
and here we are on earth.

Sometimes we wonder, God:
Why is there such pain and suffering?
Where are you in these times?

Through the great expanse of stars and sky,
Do you even see us?

We bring these questions to you,
you, in your holy temple.

We long for a day
when justice will be.

We wait for a time
when peace will be.

We yearn for the moment
when hope will be.

(prayers for justice, peace, and hope)

We are your created beings.
Not speechless idols,
nor wooden things.
You say to us, "Awake!"

From our deep slumber,
our willful unconsciousness,
with unfocused eyes,
we wake and we pray,

(prayers for the burdens on our hearts)

We are your beloved beings.
Not metal images,
nor silent stones,
You call out to us, "Arise!"

From our cushioned pews,
struggling to stand up,
yet willing to rise,
we pray,

(prayers for strength to follow Christ)

In silence, breathe into us, God,
Your church,
Your body,
Your creation.

The Lord is in his holy temple,
let all the earth keep silence before him.

Prayer After Communion
A blessing from the Eucharistic rite of the Anglican Church of Kenya

All our problems
We send them to the cross of Christ.
All our difficulties
We send them to the cross of Christ.
All the devil's works
We send them to the cross of Christ.
All our hopes
We set on the Risen Son.

May Christ the Son of Righteousness
shine upon you and
set you free from your bondage:
and the blessing of God Almighty,
Creator, Redeemer, and Holy Spirit,
be among you,
and remain with you always.
Amen.

5 DRINKING SONGS AND REMEMBERING

HABAKKUK 3.1-16

1   *A prayer of the prophet Habakkuk according to Shigionoth.*

2   *O Lord, I have heard of your renown,*
       and I stand in awe, O Lord, of your work.
    In our own time revive it;
       in our own time make it known;
       in wrath may you remember mercy.

3   *God came from Teman,*
       the Holy One from Mount Paran.

                                                    Selah

    His glory covered the heavens,
       and the earth was full of his praise.
4   *The brightness was like the sun;*
       rays came forth from his hand,
       where his power lay hidden.
5   *Before him went pestilence,*
       and plague followed close behind.
6   *He stopped and shook the earth;*
       he looked and made the nations tremble.
    The eternal mountains were shattered;
       along his ancient pathways
       the everlasting hills sank low.
7   *I saw the tents of Cushan under affliction;*
       the tent-curtains of the land of Midian trembled.

8 *Was your wrath against the rivers, O Lord?*
   Or your anger against the rivers,
   or your rage against the sea,
when you drove your horses,
   your chariots to victory?
9 *You brandished your naked bow,*
   sated were the arrows at your command.

                            Selah

   You split the earth with rivers.
10 *The mountains saw you, and writhed;*
   a torrent of water swept by;
the deep gave forth its voice.
   The sun raised high its hands;
11 *the moon stood still in its exalted place,*
   at the light of your arrows speeding by,
   at the gleam of your flashing spear.
12 *In fury you trod the earth,*
   in anger you trampled nations.
13 *You came forth to save your people,*
   to save your anointed.
You crushed the head of the wicked house,
   laying it bare from foundation to roof.

                            Selah

14 *You pierced with their own arrows*
   the head of his warriors,
   who came like a whirlwind to scatter us,
   gloating as if ready to devour the poor who were in hiding.
15 *You trampled the sea with your horses,*
   churning the mighty waters.

16 *I hear, and I tremble within;*
   my lips quiver at the sound.
Rottenness enters into my bones,
   and my steps tremble beneath me.
I wait quietly for the day of calamity
   to come upon the people who attack us.

Reflection
Singing Soul with Habakkuk
Brian Walsh

> God, I need a drink
> and I need one fast
> make it a strong one
> one that will last
> have you got anything
> that has been selling brisk
> for a soul diagnosed
> at a terminal risk?
>> ("Drunk on the Tears," Vigilantes of Love)

I think that Habakkuk would have resonated with these lines from the Vigilantes of Love.

He has seen what cheap booze can do to a soul.
He has proclaimed against the empire,
    "drink, you yourself, and stagger."
And maybe, just maybe, he's decided to have a drink or four himself.

God, I need a drink
and I need one fast.

And so the prophet who has seen it all,
    the prophet who has seen more than he can bear,
    strikes up a tune.

He breaks the silence of all the earth
    before God in his holy temple,
not simply with more words,
    but with a song.

A "Shigionoth" to be precise.
    "A prayer of the prophet Habakkuk according to Shigionoth"
is how Habakkuk 3 begins.

Of course, you know what a "Shigionoth" is, right?
    You don't?
Well, don't worry, no one really knows with any certainty.

But I'll tell you the definition that I'm going with.
    A Shigionoth is a wild, rambling song or prayer,
    perhaps under the influence of drink.

Habakkuk puts a few away
    (and who wouldn't if you had seen what he had seen?)
and starts to sing.

And, like many songs after a few drinks,
    this one gets a little nostalgic as it tells its tale.
Not quite able to grasp the reality of the present,
    the prophet reaches back to the past.
Maybe trying to ground the impossibility of hope in the present,
    and struggling with the unlikelihood
    of this tragic oracle turning out well,
the prophet sings of the stories that are at the very root of his being,
    the very ground of his community.

Can I believe that you will overcome the violent Chaldeans?
Well, you overcame the Egyptian empire in the past.

But the nostalgia won't work,
and, as happens so often in this ancient version
of the "soul music" genre,
nostalgia gives way to melancholy at best,
despair at worse.

In the end our singer confesses:

    "I hear, and I tremble within;
    my lips quiver at the sound.
    Rottenness enters into my bones,
    and my steps tremble beneath me.
    I wait quietly for the day of calamity,
    to come upon the people who attack us."

Not exactly a song of triumph.
Not a song to rally the troops.
Not really where the praise band wanted to leave us.

The song that was supposed to instill confidence
    leaves the singer trembling with quivering lips,
    stumbling forward on unsure feet.

Dear friends, I know that quivering lips,
a profound sense of inner disquiet and dis-ease,
and stumbling, unsure feet,
are well known in our midst.

Many of us find ourselves singing the old story;
    indeed, even deeply believing that story,
and yet singing through tears,
    trying our hardest to hold it together,
not knowing where our life is going,
    or what the next steps might be.

And I know that it has been painful and dangerous
    for some of us to see what Habakkuk has seen,
    and to feel what he has felt.

So why go there?

Well, because maybe, just maybe,
    grief is the doorway to hope,
    lament is the path to liberation,
    and death opens to resurrection.

If none of this is true,
    then I am sorry.
We should have never opened up Habakkuk.

But if it is true, then we need to face the grief,
    give anguished voice to our lament,
    and stare all that is deathly straight in the face,
hanging from this high wire by the tatters of our faith,
    believing against the evidence,
that life is stronger than death,
    hope is stronger than despair,
and that the just will live by faith.

I don't know if you can believe this.
    But I'll tell you this:
you can't believe it on your own.
    And that is why we have something as audacious as
Wine Before Breakfast so early on a Tuesday morning.

Musical/Liturgical Comment
Deb Whalen-Blaize

In all of this waiting – waiting for action; waiting for justice; waiting for restoration; waiting to rise up – it's easy to feel disconnected – from situations to people. Even from those we love. Even from those we believe love us. In light of all this destruction, I get the sense that Habakkuk is feeling a deep sense of disconnection. All through this oracle, he questions God and begs for him to account for everything that's going on.

> Destruction everywhere, God! Why?
> Injustice and suffering among the righteous, God! Why?
> The earth is crumbling, God! Why?

Disconnection can leave you feeling out at sea. Far removed. Grief-stricken. Powerless. Lost. It fills you with the blues and kinda leaves you there. There is an entire genre of music that was born out of this kind of sadness and disenfranchisement. So we began our service with the blues and sang the old gospel blues song "Motherless Child." We took our cue for the arrangement from Van Morrison – his drawn-out phrasing of these yearning words makes you feel rather than simply hear this song. I am especially moved by the last verse, for all the tension that's in it, and I can easily imagine Habakkuk singing this to himself:

> Sometimes I feel like freedom is near
> But we're so far from home

But from somewhere out there, we hear the call to worship. Or perhaps it's from that cavernous place deep inside us that the call comes. So we responded with "Come Thou Fount of Every Blessing." Despite all of the threatening images in the text for this service, this hymn held us together in a resolve:

> Here I make faith's affirmation
> Thus far by thy help I've come
> And I hope by thy compassion
> Safely to arrive at home

This hymn offered us a way forward in the darkness and desolation. From there we put the melody of "Amazing Grace" to the words of the hymn "Come, Let Us to the Lord Our God." This hymn resonated well with the awesome power of God in all of creation proclaimed by Habakkuk in this week's text.

His voice commands the tempest forth
And stills the stormy wave
And though his arm be strong to smite
'Tis also strong to save

The voice that calls the cleansing tempest from the heavens is the same voice that commands it to halt. That same arm, so easily swung into violence and wrath, can also reach through the terror and pluck us from danger. Often we wish he'd swoop in with that rescue a lot sooner than he does, but salvation has come, and if God is, indeed, faithful, then that salvific hand must be on its way again. And so Habakkuk implores God: "O Lord, I have heard of your renown, and I stand in awe, O Lord, of your work. In your own time, revive it; in our own time make it known; in wrath may you remember mercy."

Sure, Habakkuk feels the need to remind God of his capacity for mercy amidst the wrath he is calling down – but he has faith that it is still there. Because "though his arm be strong to smite, 'tis also strong to save." Always strong to save.

During communion we sang The Vineyard's "I Cry Out." I love the last stanza of this song especially, where over and over we get to sing "For you are good, for you are good, for you are good to me." I grew up singing this song at summer camp, at night around the campfire. I learned this song in the dark and found a refuge in that refrain that comes to me from time to time, when I find myself in dark times.

We also sang the old gospel tune "Let Us Break Bread Together," committing to breaking bread, drinking the wine, and praising God together on our knees. In hope and submission and full awareness that we are not in control, we broke the body of our Lord, drank his cup of joy, and praised him. There is so much going on in our lives that we cannot control. Sometimes we, like the prophet, can feel like it is all destruction. That's where the resolve comes in. Often we have to resolve to more than just one thing: resolve to wait on God; to worship him; to commit to and contribute to justice; to not allow ourselves to waste away, rottenness entering our bones. Perhaps God wants to do his work through us as we carry out these commitments and acts of resolution. And we are empowered to his good work at the table of the Eucharist, nurtured by Christ's body and blood.

If we are to go out and try to spread some light and embolden the down-hearted stuck in the darkness, we must find a balance. Somewhere between getting stuck in the mire of hopelessness and the oblivion of pretending nothing's wrong. This tension sent us right back to the blues of Mr. Van Morrison, and so we sang the service to a close with his song "Stranded."

> I'm stranded between that ol' devil and the deep blue sea
> And nobody's gonna tell me what time it is
>
> Every day it's hustle time
> Every day, and every way, one more mountain to climb

Van Morrison knows what it means to not have the end in sight. So we sang through those blues, accepting that this is a real place in our lives. It can be dark. It can be threatening. It can be chaotic and confusing and completely blindsiding. So often we are left feeling stranded. And so we must continue to cling to that hope that God's arm is fully capable and willing to save. We must cling to that feeling that freedom is near, despite being so far from home. And sometimes the best way to do that is to find the right blues tune and allow our hearts to beat along in time, and allow the melody to carry us forward.

> I cry out for your hand of mercy to heal me
> I am weak and I need your love to free me
> O Lord, my rock, my strength in weakness
> Come rescue me, O Lord
>
> You are my rock, your promise never fails me
> And my desire is to follow you forever
> For you are good, for you are good
> For you are good to me
> For you are good, for you are good
> For you are good to me

* * *

> Let us break bread together on our knees
> Let us break bread together on our knees
> When I fall on my knees with my face to the rising sun
> O Lord have mercy on me
>
> Let us drink wine together on our knees
> Let us drink wine together on our knees
> When I fall on my knees with my face to the rising sun
> O Lord have mercy on me

Prelude	Motherless Child *African American spiritual, with some Van Morrison*
Postlude	Stranded *Van Morrison*
Hymns	Come Thou Fount of Every Blessing *#354*
	Come, Let Us to the Lord Our God *#607; to the tune of "Amazing Grace"*
	I Cry Out *Craig Musseau*
	Let Us Break Bread Together *African American spiritual*

Let us serve God together on our knees
Let us serve God together on our knees
When I fall on my knees with my face to the rising sun
O Lord have mercy on me

The Gathering of the Community

Brian Walsh

God I need a drink,
and I need one fast.
**Make it a strong one,
one that will last.**

Have you got something
that's been selling brisk,
**for a soul diagnosed
at a terminal risk?**

It's been my staple
for so many years,
it's hard to taste the wine,
when you're drunk on the tears.

Let us pray.
Lord, we're stranded,
staggering and stumbling,
lips quivering,
and the rot of death is deep within us.

Come!
Save!
Heal!
We're so hungry,
and we're so thirsty.

Homily
Let the Saxophone Wail
Andrew Federle

Grover Sales

I took a course in university called The History of Jazz. I signed up for it because I thought it would be an easy elective. Instead, I walked away with a C-, which was essentially the equivalent of an F where I went to school. When they give you a C-, what they are really saying is, "Are you *sure* university is where you're meant to be?"

The exams for the course involved listening to a series of vintage jazz recordings and trying to discern which instrument was playing at the time: was that a saxophone or a clarinet? A trombone or a tuba? And I got a C- because I never could tell. I never could remember.

The course was taught by a flailing scarecrow of a man named Grover Sales. Sales, who was white, made a childhood out of sneaking into black jazz clubs while he was still underage. It was there that he fell in love with jazz and blues music. Although I never could remember which instrument Sales was talking about, I will never forget one thing he said, which is that Gospel and blues music both flow from exactly the same place. It's just that one sings "Jesus" while the other sings "Baby." Same tune, different lyrics.

Present Tense

The prophet Habakkuk remembers the lyrics:

> O LORD, I have heard of your renown, and I stand in awe, O LORD, of your work. In our own time revive it; in our own time make it known; in wrath may you remember mercy.

Habakkuk remembers the days when God's works were manifold and mighty. He remembers the days before God seemed to go silent. Because now it all seemed to be ashes and wrath.

And his mind trails off … he stumbles a bit and grabs a chair. He sits down and pours himself a stiff drink ….

I once took John Campbell, the former music director for Church of the Redeemer, out for a drink. And somehow we got to talking about the Psalms. And he told me that anytime you come across the notation *Selah*, it means "Let the saxophone wail."

Selah

A musician from the band plays his trumpet. Andrew takes a drink of wine, after which he sings:

> Sometimes I feel like a motherless child
> Sometimes I feel like a motherless child
> Sometimes I feel like a motherless child
> A long way from my home

Mount Sinai

When he opens his eyes again, Habakkuk is no longer in the present. He is remembering the place where he first heard the good news:

> I am the LORD your God who brought you up out of the land our Egypt, out of the house of slavery.

And then the images in this prophecy begin to pile, one upon another:

> Before him went pestilence, and plague followed close behind. He stopped and shook the earth; he looked and made the nations tremble. The eternal mountains were shattered; along his ancient pathways the everlasting hills sank low.

The thunder and the lightning, the pestilence and the plague of deliverance. All of these are evocative of the revelation of God's presence at Mount Sinai: God's promise to be the God of this people, and to lead them from the place of slavery into the land of promise.

In Judaism, this covenant is remembered yearly at the Festival of Weeks. This festival celebrates the anniversary of the revelation at Sinai. It is a remembrance of a foundational time when God was present and God's fierce loyalty was felt.

Selah

A musician from the band plays his trumpet. Andrew takes a drink of wine, after which he sings:

> Motherless children have a hard time
> Motherless children have a – such a hard time
> Motherless children have such a really hard time
> A long way from home

Exodus

Habakkuk opens his eyes once more, and this time he's back – even further now – in the midst of the Exodus. And he remembers God's fury, when all of creation conspired to get Israel the hell out of Egypt – mountains, sun, moon, waters, all pulling for the people of God:

> You crushed the head of the wicked house, laying it bare from foundation to roof.... You pierced with his own arrows the head of his warriors, who came like a whirlwind to scatter us, gloating as if ready to devour the poor who were in hiding. You trampled the sea with your horses, churning the mighty waters."

The people of Israel were stuck between the devil and the deep blue sea. The Egyptians on one side and the Red Sea on the other. Where are you going to go? You're going to go through the waters. Not around them, but through them.

Selah

A musician from the band plays his trumpet. Andrew takes a drink of wine, after which he sings:

> Sometimes I feel like freedom is near
> Sometimes I feel like freedom is here

Sometimes I feel like freedom is so near
But we're so far from home

Present Again

Habakkuk comes to from his drinking song … and he is back where he began. Back in the present. Same circumstances … same tune … different lyrics:

> I wait quietly for the day of calamity to come upon the people who attack us.

This is the mercy. A place of quiet in the midst of destruction.

Having remembered the mountain of revelation, and the sea of deliverance, Habakkuk can now face the day of destruction. Having remembered, he is now able to face the full reality of his awful situation. And to *know*, in his bones, that he cannot do an end run around it. He must pass *through* it. Knowing God is with him all the same.

Sometimes that is enough.

Prayers of the People
Jacqueline Daley

O Lord, I have heard of your renown,
and I stand in awe, O Lord, of your work.
In our own time revive it;
in our own time make it known;
in wrath may you remember mercy.

This is our story;
this is our song,
our song of pain,
our song of lament,
our song of radical hope and praise
in the midst of our suffering.

(silent and spoken prayers for ourselves and those who need mercy)

His glory covered the heavens,
and the earth was full of his praise.

The brightness was like the sun;
rays came forth from his hand,
where his power lay hidden.

You split the earth with rivers.
The mountains saw you, and writhed;
a torrent of water swept by;
the deep gave forth its voice.

The sun raised high its hands;
the moon stood still in its exalted place,
at the light of your arrows speeding by,
at the gleam of your flashing spear.
I hear, and I tremble within;
my lips quiver at the sound.

This is our story;
this is our song,
our song of pain,
our song of lament,
our song of radical hope and praise
in the midst of our suffering.

(silent and spoken prayers for the world)

Though the fig tree does not blossom,
and no fruit is on the vines;
though the produce of the olive fails,
and the fields yield no food;
though the flock is cut off from the fold,
and there is no herd in the stalls,
yet I will rejoice in the Lord;
I will exult in the God of my salvation.

God, the Lord, is my strength;
he makes my feet like the feet of a deer,
and makes me tread upon the heights.

This is our story;
this is our song,
our song of pain,

our song of lament,
our song of radical hope and praise
in the midst of our suffering.

And in the face of it all we are still bold to say,
Glory to God,
whose power, working in us
can do infinitely more
than we can ask or imagine.
Glory to God from generation to generation,
in the Church and in Christ Jesus,
for ever and ever. Amen.

6 THE LIBERATING *YET*

HABAKKUK 3.17-19

17 *Though the fig tree does not blossom,*
   and no fruit is on the vines;
   though the produce of the olive fails,
   and the fields yield no food;
   though the flock is cut off from the fold,
   and there is no herd in the stalls,
18 *yet I will rejoice in the Lord;*
   I will exult in the God of my salvation.
19 *God, the Lord, is my strength;*
   he makes my feet like the feet of a deer,
   and makes me tread upon the heights.

   To the leader: with stringed instruments.

Reflection
You Got Me Singing
Brian Walsh

"To the leader: with stringed instruments."

Those are the last lines in the prophecy of Habakkuk.

Habakkuk has seen as much as he can handle.
This oracle has been to him a burden.

It's been bad,
it's been painful,
it's been frightening,
    these past weeks in Habakkuk.

The prophet saw with a devastating clarity:
    the judgment of God,
    the calamity of history,
    the implosion of empire,
    the toppling of idols.

And somehow seeing through his ancient eyes,
    we have been brought more deeply into the
    judgment, calamity, implosion, and toppling
        of our own time,
        of our own lives.

He had seen enough,
    and so, after a few stiff drinks,
    he launched into a song.

Perhaps with a touch of inebriated melancholy
    the prophet sings a story that should cheer him up,
    but he finds himself with quivering lips,
    trembling, feeling sick to his core,
    and he begins to stumble.

Anyone know that experience?

Seems to me that I see something like this every Tuesday morning.

So what do you do?
What do you do when a story of joy leaves you in a puddle of tears?
What do you do when all the news is bad?
What do you do when your world has fallen apart?
What do you do when you don't know if you can still believe?
What do you do when you are so deeply disappointed
    in God,
    in God's people,
    in yourself?

Well, you believe against the evidence,
    and the only way that I know how to do that
    is through singing.

Habakkuk sings,
    "*though* the fig tree does not blossom,
        and no fruit is on the vines,
    though the produce of the olive fails
        and the fields yield no food;
    though the flock is cut off from the fold
        and there is no herd in the stalls,
    yet I will rejoice in the Lord;
        I will exult in the God of my salvation.
    God, the Lord is my strength;
        he makes my feet like the feet of a deer,
        and makes me tread upon the heights.

    To the leader: with stringed instruments."

This isn't stuff that you can simply say.
    As if saying these words over and over to yourself,
        maybe conjuring up some good arguments,
        maybe praying these words like a mantra
    will ever be enough,
    will ever make any of this believable.

No, my friends, we only can access this kind of faith,
    this kind of in-your-face,
    audacious and radical hope,
        by singing it,
        by allowing this song to set you free,
        by allowing the tune to resonate even more deeply in you
        than the terrible visions that we have seen.

In his iconic anthem, "Hallelujah," Leonard Cohen put it this way:

> "And even though it all went wrong,
> I'll stand before the Lord of song,
> with nothing on my tongue
> but 'Hallelujah!'"

And now, so many years later, Cohen is still singing:

> "You got me singing,
> Even though it all looks grim,
> You got me singing,
> The Hallelujah hymn."

And so we end our sojourn with Habakkuk
   the only place it could end.

In song.

Musical/Liturgical Comment
Deb Whalen-Blaize

Over the last five weeks we had engaged most of Habakkuk's disturbing words in his book of prophecy. Our final week left us looking at these last three verses that, frankly, don't come to the kind of closure most of us like. After weeks as a community, watching and waiting for this prophet in his watching and waiting, we find a defiant resolution to sing praise in spite of it all. Habakkuk doesn't prophesy a happy ending to all of this. In fact, he doesn't prophesy an ending at all. He will go on, resolved in his waiting.

And that's life, isn't it? We find that the waiting and the resolution are a constant process. We will always be waiting on God. We will always be waiting for deliverance as justice is threatened, and we will always be caught in the crossfire. We can't actually remove ourselves from the action, try as we may. And so I began looking for "swan songs," so to speak: songs that spoke of our understanding and awareness of this constant waiting. We wait now, and we will always be waiting. We resolve to believe in God's faithfulness, no matter how difficult it is to believe while we wait. And unfortunately there is absolutely nothing we can do to provoke God into action. So we resolve to wait and to hope until we see him act.

Glen Hansard's "Falling Slowly" is an anthem for the weary who refuse to give up. That would be us.

> Take this sinking boat and point it home
> We've still got time
> Raise your hopeful voice, you have a choice
> You've made it now
>
> Falling slowly, sing your melody
> I'll sing it loud

The water imagery, the words of hope, the acknowledgment and acceptance that things do not look good, all add up to a very gritty and yet somehow heartening song. Like the prophet, the artist insists "I'll sing it loud" in the face of the evidence. The song evokes the camaraderie we need to get through. If one person is singing in those last drowning moments, wouldn't it be heartening to hear a little harmony? Sometimes our support of one another is all we have as we wait and watch and hope. What better way to rally people's spirits than to sing together? And in that community the artist sings, "I hear you. I've got you. I'm singing along."

So we joined our voices, loudly, to sing a hymn of hope in the face of the crisis we had been sitting in for so many weeks. A song of hope and rebuilding, "My Hope Is Built on Nothing Less," was clearly the song for us to sing.

> On Christ the solid rock I stand
> All other ground is sinking sand

We may have entered into this period of lament and reflection with Habakkuk but we never took our eyes off of Jesus. Yes, we wait for our individual and corporate challenges to be resolved and our patience to be rewarded by seeing justice come to fruition, but Jesus opens our eyes to see that in all things God's goodness is more powerful than any destruction, impending or otherwise. The sacrificial love that we meet in Jesus overcomes any offspring of evil. Despite the mess evil leaves in its wake, Jesus is our example that nothing can overcome love. Messiah Jesus shows us that love's power is worth our faith, hope, and patience. Christ endured all kinds of violence and injustice, yielded to it completely, so he could show up a few days later and prove that even death is not the end of the

story. Evil does not have the final say. You have to admire guys like Habakkuk, who were fighting the good fight prior to the revolutionary story
of Jesus. What kind of chutzpa does it take to confess, "Yet I will rejoice
in the Lord" in the face of death-inducing destruction and barrenness?

And so our following hymns centred on sticking close to God, the source
of life and love. In "Guide Me, O Thou Great Jehovah," William Williams
employs images of barrenness and devastation to contrast and prove
God's strength. I love the line "I am weak, but thou art mighty / hold
me with thy powerful hand." Not "take me up and rescue me from the
situation I'm in." Not "whisk me away and get me off the hook." But "be
thou my strength and shield" in the fray, in the struggle. We rely on God's
strength in order to find our own. God's strength sustains us in situations
where our own strength is not enough.

"Guide Me, O Thou Great Jehovah" takes us to the table: "bread of
heaven, feed me till I want no more." And communion is the perfect time
to reflect on the sustenance we find through Christ's nourishment. At
Wine Before Breakfast, the Eucharist table is at the very heart of our faith
practice. Everything we do is sustained from the nourishment we find at
Christ's table. We break bread and drink wine at every service as if our
life depended on it. We must be sustained by the body and blood of Jesus
if we are to carry out our commitment to making the kingdom of God
known in our everyday lives.

As we shared communion together we sang "All Who Hunger."

All who hunger, sing together;
Jesus Christ is living bread.
Come from loneliness and longing.
Here, in peace, we have been led.
Blest are those who from this table,
live their lives in gratitude.
Taste and see the grace eternal.
Taste and see that God is good.

Once again, we are reminded that this isn't just a matter of our personal
relationships with God. Its bigger than you or me. Together, in Christ, we
are all building this kingdom of justice. We are Christ's followers, nour-
ished at his table. We will see and find God's strength and love in our
brothers and sisters. And when our hope is dying, the spark of another's
faith can sometimes reignite us. This is why we stick together. We are the
face of God to one another. You cannot strengthen your relationship with
God and not grow in your relationship to others. Together, we are more

Prelude	Falling Slowly *Glen Hansard and Markéta Irglová*
Postlude	You Got Me Singing *Leonard Cohen*
Hymns	My Hope Is Built on Nothing Less *Edward Mote*
	Guide Me, O Thou Great Jehovah *#565*
	All Who Hunger *Sylvia Dunstan*

likely to taste and see God's goodness, know his strength and stand up against the injustice in our lives.

It is this strength and love of God that keeps us from losing the plot and just drowning in the mire. Having experienced again God's love and commitment, we can stand together at the end of it all with Habakkuk and sing, "Yet I will rejoice in the Lord."

So, it was no surprise that we ended where we began. With Leonard Cohen. Cohen's album *Popular Problems* had been released just a few months prior to our journey with Habakkuk and there we found the gorgeous song that would provide us with the perfect end to our sojourn with this prophet. Cohen gets Habakkuk.

Our journey began with Cohen's "Anthem." There we sang for those who have a weary longing for justice, for life in the face of death. "Anthem" was a song that called us to ring the bells that still can ring, and to forget our perfect offerings. If we thought that we had any such perfect offerings at the beginning of our time with Habakkuk, we had been seriously disabused of the notion by the end.

But Cohen insists that devoid of any perfect offerings, we still have voices, we still have a song to sing. And so we brought it all to a close with his song "You Got Me Singing." And this song is perfect for a community like us. A people who do not gloss over the difficulty and destruction in the world, but who know the love and power of God, who not only will answer, but has answered. He is coming, but he is also with us. Already. Here, now. And will always be. The God we meet at Wine Before Breakfast, the God we meet in Habakkuk, and the God who takes on flesh in Jesus is not separated from the suffering. He is in the midst of it. He endures it with us. God's commitment to us is what keeps us singing. "Even though the news is bad," "ever since the river died," "even though the world is gone," God has got us singing and thinking that we'd "like to carry on."

And that is quite the thing. It would be easier, somehow, to just give up, or to avert our eyes from the pain within and without, but both Jewish prophets – Habakkuk and Leonard Cohen – invite us to keep singing "the Hallelujah hymn."

My hope is built on nothing less,
Than Jesus' blood and righteousness.
I dare not trust the sweetest frame,
But wholly trust in Jesus' Name.

Refrain
On Christ the solid Rock I stand,
All other ground is sinking sand;
All other ground is sinking sand.

When darkness seems to hide His face,
I rest on His unchanging grace.
In every high and stormy gale,
My anchor holds within the veil.

Refrain

His oath, His covenant, His blood,
Support me in the whelming flood.
When all around my soul gives way,
He then is all my Hope and Stay.

Refrain

When He shall come with trumpet sound,
Oh may I then in Him be found.
Dressed in His righteousness alone,
Faultless to stand before the throne.

Refrain

***

All who hunger, gather gladly;
holy manna is our bread.
Come from wilderness and wandering.
Here, in truth, we will be fed.
You that yearn for days of fullness,
all around us is our food.
Taste and see the grace eternal.
Taste and see that God is good.

All who hunger, never strangers;
seeker, be a welcome guest.
Come from restlessness and roaming.
Here, in joy, we keep the feast.
We that once were lost and scattered,
in communion's love have stood.
Taste and see the grace eternal.
Taste and see that God is good.

All who hunger, sing together;
Jesus Christ is living bread.
Come from loneliness and longing.
Here, in peace, we have been led.
Blest are those who from this table,
live their lives in gratitude.
Taste and see the grace eternal.
Taste and see that God is good.

The Gathering of the Community

Amanda Jagt

Some days
we sing new songs.
Some days
we sing old songs.
Some days
we sing songs of sorrow.
Some days
we sing songs of joy.

This day,
in the face of violence and war,
in the face of injustice and degradation,
in the face of apathy and greed,
we come to raise hopeful voices;
we come to sing as many and as one;
we come to be pointed toward home.

Homily
Wrestlers at the End
Beth Carlson-Malena

Lately I've caught myself thinking a lot about the End.

Which is weird, because I've actually had a lot of beginnings
  in my life lately.
  Just nine months ago, I married my wife.
    Just six months ago, we moved from Vancouver to Toronto.
      A new city, with my new wife, to start new jobs.
        … with an organization called New Direction.
          So, lots of "new."

But for some reason, I can't help thinking about the End.
  More specifically, the End of the World.

Maybe I'm feeling apocalyptic because of these violent
  fringe religious groups, like ISIS.
    Some days I wonder how we've gone this long
      without some fanatic nuking our planet.

Or maybe it's hearing my environmental activist friends change their tone,
  from "Let's stop climate change!"
  to "Too late, we're past the point of no return."

I may also be thinking about the end of the world
  because I'm hooked on a certain TV show called "The Walking Dead."
    Anyone else?
      Honestly, I could take or leave the zombies
      – they don't really do it for me.

What keeps me coming back
    is watching how the human survivors actually survive.
        How they learn to rely on people who had been total strangers to them,
            trying to decide whom to trust and include in their group,
            and whom to avoid.

Every time they suffer another betrayal, another death,
    it makes them a little colder, more vengeful, less human.
        I keep watching to see if they can hold on to their humanity.
It's hard to stay human when your world is ending.
    When all of a sudden, instead of worrying about
    whether you should invest in the newest iPhone,
        you're worrying about whether you will wake up tomorrow.

Maybe you've hit a point like that already in your life,
    When it felt like all was lost. Nothing mattered.

Today we're at an ending – the end of Habakkuk.
    There's a double meaning there.
        It's the end of the book, and it also very well could be
            the end of the man.
        Because, frankly, things aren't looking good for Habakkuk.

    Habakkuk's name also has a double meaning.
        It's from the Hebrew word *Chabak*,
            meaning "one who embraces" or "one who wrestles."

So far we've seen Habakkuk the wrestler,
    the prophet who dared to wrestle with God.
        Dared to call God out for ignoring injustice,
            dared to question why God would use Babylon,
            an even wickeder people, to restore justice.
        He will not sit down and accept pat answers.
            The wrestler will not let go until he gets a blessing.

In this third chapter, his wrestling partner, Yahweh, stands up, and shakes
    the earth.
    Splits the rivers, churns the waters, throws lightning bolts,
        and generally reminds Habakkuk that he is hopelessly outmatched.

And now,
    after sweeping visions of swiftly approaching armies,
        and of this warrior God,

Habakkuk is left alone, heart racing, lips trembling,
    so unsteady his bones could snap.

He could try to run, but he doesn't.
    He chooses to wait for the disaster.
        As he waits, Habakkuk looks around himself at the land of Judah,
            and sees a vision – present or future, we don't know.

What he sees are fig trees, vines, olive trees – all barren.
    Crops in the fields – the food for the rest of the year – all dead.
        Even the last resort – the cattle and sheep,
            the ones you only butcher and eat if all else fails – they're gone, too.

In other words, the investments have gone south,
    the savings account is tapped,
        the chequing account is empty,
            even the emergency cash
                in that envelope under your mattress has disappeared.

But that doesn't capture the extent of the hopelessness here,
    because what Habakkuk is describing is not just economic collapse,
        but also, symbolically, the total spiritual collapse of a people.

Because the people of Judah *are* the vine God is tending,
    but the vine has no grapes.
        They *are* the flock of sheep God is shepherding,
            but they've wandered off.

The blessing has turned to curse.
    This is total economic and spiritual bankruptcy.
        This is the End.

What is Habakkuk supposed to do at the end?
    This is not his fault!
        He's the prophet, the righteous one, living by faith.
            Why should *he* be punished for his people's evil?

It's too bad. The Babylonians are coming with a vengeance,
    and something tells me they're not going to pause
        and decide which Judean deserves to live or die.
            Habakkuk will get caught in the crossfire.

And I wonder if, at the End,
    standing in a dry field full of dead vines and shrivelled trees,
        Habakkuk may have admitted to some of his own shrivelled-ness.

Miroslav Volf says,
> "The harder I pursue justice, the blinder I become
> to the injustice I myself perpetuate."

I slam the racist white Americans in Ferguson,
> and wake up to a *Maclean's* article about racial inequality in my own backyard.

I bash Harper for failing to limit carbon emissions,
> but I can't even limit my own consumption, or my own greed.

A movie about an unabashed sniper of Muslims gets more nominations
> than one about a nonviolent African American martyr,
> > and I feel the rage rising in my own throat,
> > > the violent rage of a sniper, not a martyr.

I'm pretty damn good at diagnosing fear, prejudice, and anger,
> but it doesn't change the fact that I'm still a carrier of the disease.
> > It's in me, too.

Even prophets can't completely wrest themselves from the death-dealing systems.
> None are righteous.
> > We all stand condemned
> > > in the middle of a barren field with Habakkuk,
> > > > and now the End can't come quickly enough.

But it's here, right in Habakkuk's bleakest of all moments,
> that we find the "*Yet*."
> > *Yet* I will rejoice in the Lord.
> > > *Yet*, that three-letter turning point – only one letter in the Hebrew.
> > > Not much of a hinge.

Does that verse bug you? Does it rub itself in your face?
> Habakkuk simply moves from verse 17 to verse 18,
> > giving us no clue of *how* to get from the famine to the joy.

> > It's one thing to wait and be stoic in the face of disaster,
> > > But it's another thing to be joyful as disaster comes.
> > > Sounds almost masochistic.

With this impending doom, how can we possibly muster up joy and worship?
> That takes more strength than we have right now.

Unless that's just it.
   Unless being absolutely spent, fingers slipping off the rope,
   helpless to help ourselves,
      is the only way to get to the "yet."

After all, wasn't it our self-reliance that got us into this mess in the first place?

The God who crumbles the ancient mountains with his footsteps
   is willing to make us stand like a nimble deer on the heights.
      We just have to be weak enough to let him be our strength.
      Doomed enough to let him be the God of our salvation.

When every earthly prop gives way, he then is all my hope and stay.

We've been wrestling this God, holding him accountable;
   wrestling this evil in our people, this evil in ourselves;
      and this is good. We're not called to passivity, to the bliss of ignorance.

But Habakkuk has a two-part name
   – the one who wrestles is also the one who embraces.
      He's a lover and a fighter.
      And a wrestling hold sure looks a lot like an embrace.

Can we lean on this God we're wrestling?
   This God with whom we are gloriously outmatched?
      Can we trust the character of the God of our salvation,
        and embrace him at the end,
          even if we don't understand his methods or his timing?

I think this is our only hope. This is the source of our humanity.

So, prophets, let's climb down from our watchtower for a moment.
   Let's stand in a barren and bankrupt country,
      right in the midst of the sinful people we've been rebuking,
      you know, the ones hooking and dragging people in their nets,
        the ones who do violence to each other and to the earth,
          all those zombies like us,
          all these motherless children.

With the hooves of the Babylonian horses already stomping in the distance,
   let's sing the blues, let's confess together
      that we don't know what to do. We can't fix this. It's *in* us.

And in that moment when we are completely spent,
    will we notice a hint of gospel creeping into our song?
        Same tune, different lyrics.

Will our songs weave themselves into a delicate hope,
    might we start to make out the deep undertones
        of our divine wrestling partner joining the song,
            whispering that when we think it's the end,
                it's never really the end?

Because nothing can separate us from his love.
    Death can't. Life can't.
        Even after the armies, the famine, the disaster, the apocalypse,
        he will never abandon us, never leave us alone.
        He has more for us.

Even now he might give us a taste, like a muted trumpet of victory,
    whisking us up like a deer up on the hills, where he alone treads,
        where the enemy can't reach us,
        where we get a bird's eye view of his plan.

So call up the director of music
and tell him to round up the stringed instruments.
    Disaster is coming, but we're not running away.
        We're not averting our eyes.
        We will **embrace** this.
            Heck, we will **rejoice** in this.

Because until all is well,
    and all is well,
        and all manner of things is well,
            it is not yet finished.
            It is not yet the end.

Prayers of the People

Amanda Jagt

O Lord, O Choirmaster,
though the fig tree should not blossom,
you got us singing.

Though we had a dream that was not all a dream,
you got us singing.

Though the sedge is withered from the lake,
you got us singing.

Though our eyes are full of things wept and unwept,
you got us singing.

Though we are sick, tired, and anxious,
you got us singing.

Though no cattle low from the pasturelands,
you got us singing.

You got us singing:
Give us strength
   to hope.
Give us strength
   to have faith.
Give us strength
   to love.
Give us strength
   to work for justice and peace.

(silent and spoken prayers and songs)

You got us singing
because love will save this place.

You got us singing
because you, O God, are our strength.

You got us singing
because Christ is our living bread.

You got us singing
because rose-moles are stippled upon trout that swim.

You got us singing
because the Kingdom is like a mustard seed.

You got us singing
because you make our feet like the deer's.

She treads on high places;
on rocky cliffs she climbs,
and in these places,
of which it was said there is only waste and desolation,
of which it was said there is neither hope nor joy,
there will be heard the guitar and the drum,
the piano, the trumpet, and the shaker;
there will be heard the voice of mirth and gladness;
there will be heard singing.

(silent and spoken prayers and songs)

Even though the news is bad,
you got us singing the only song we ever had.
Even though the world is gone,
you got us thinking we'd like to carry on.
Even though it all looks grim,
you got us singing this hallelujah hymn.
Amen.

Prayer After Communion
A prayer from John Philip Newell

For the freshness of this new day
thanks be to you, O God.
For morning's gift of clarity,
its light like the first day's dawn,
thanks be to you.
In this newborn light
let us see afresh.
In this gateway onto what has never been before
let our souls breathe hope
for the earth
for the creatures
for the human family.
Let our souls breathe hope.

And in hope we say,
**Glory to God,
whose power, working in us
can do infinitely more
than we can ask or imagine.
Glory to God from generation to generation,
in the Church and in Christ Jesus,
for ever and ever. Amen.**

CPSIA information can be obtained
at www.ICGtesting.com
Printed in the USA
JSHW011557090220
4073JS00002B/77